STUDIES IN AMERICAN LITERATURE

Volume XX

☆☆☆☆☆☆☆☆☆☆☆☆☆☆☆☆☆☆☆☆☆☆☆☆☆☆☆☆☆☆☆☆☆☆

AMERICAN NOVELS
OF THE
SECOND WORLD WAR

by

JOSEPH J. WALDMEIR

1969

MOUTON

THE HAGUE · PARIS

For My Wife

Bless Her Patience

This war is not merely about a lot of guys. ... It is about a lot of guys who are doing something which will have significance when their uniforms are moth eaten and don't fit anymore. ... Something which is not human is growing in the air between our soldiers, and between them and the enemy, and between them and our allies. This non-human – in a sense, unreportable – thing is real, however. It is a real part of the truth. And it is, to me and to my children, the important fact about this war. They will not be affected by how GI Joe managed to bathe out of a helmet, but their lives will be warped or enriched according to the way that non-human quantity develops now. That quantity goes by the name, idea. I know that the very word has been made to seem naïve when used in relation to our soldiers, but if the picture were to leave out the ideas being born in this war, and the ideas being destroyed in this war, I insist that what remained would be a meaningless pantomine of bloodshed, a weird witches' tale without sense or consequence.

Arthur Miller, *Situation Normal*, 1944.

PREFACE

A World War II novel is one in which the war – on land or sea or in the air, in any branch of the services, in any theater of operations or on the home front – plays an integral, motivational, decisive role. Literally hundreds of novels in more than a dozen languages fit this definition; World War II was perhaps the most painstakingly recorded war, in fiction at least, of all time. Therefore, any unlimited discussion of the war novel as genre would be at best an annotated bibliography, and at worst a series of cross references.

But I found that the problems of limitation were not easily solved. The first step was relatively simple: to limit the discussion only to those novels in which combat, actually or in retrospect, figures prominently. The second step was more difficult to take since it seemed somewhat less reasonable than the first: to include only those novels written by and about Americans. A great many very good English, French, German, Russian, and Japanese novels are thereby excluded: but necessity dictated the decision, and it is not unusual after all to concentrate on the literary production of only one nation during a given time. But even after these two limitations were imposed, I was faced with some 250 novels which qualified for inclusion in the discussion. Obviously, a third step needed to be taken.

Besides being American combat novels, those 250 had something else in common: they were all, implicitly or explicitly, pro-war novels; that is, their authors clearly were committed to the war, sufficiently at least that in no novel was it condemned as useless or senseless as the first World War had frequently been condemned by its chroniclers. In many cases indeed, the authors dealt with the ideological issues in the war, and focussed on its political, moral, and ethical causes and consequences. With some hesitation, I took the third step in limitation toward these explicitly ideological novels.

The step is logical and defensible; all other things being equal, these novels have more to say about the war than those which do not deal in ideas. Still, I made the decision with many misgivings. Again, as in the case of the non-American novels, many excellent books would be excluded – possibly even in favor of some not nearly as good though more "ideological". Furthermore, this approach put me in the unfortunate position of having to categorize the novels, and categories are never really very satisfactory; they refuse to hold still, and they tend to flow into and through one another. In these terms, the weakness of John T. Fredericks' organization of the novels into (1) those attempting to present the total experience of a major phase of the war, (2) those dealing with experience in a single branch of service over an extended area of time and action, and (3) those limited in focus to a brief time and relatively few characters is obvious. Just as obvious is the tenuousness of Chester Eisinger's division of the novels according to Patterns of Despair and Patterns of Affirmation. But my own division of the novels into those concerned primarily with a realistic portrayal of combat, those which are principally studies of the effects of war upon an individual psyche, and those which are above all else ideological is not significantly more substantial than Frederick's or Eisinger's. It is however, more useful, if one is concerned with limiting his discussion within the boundaries of a total body of work and with getting at at least one coherent aspect of the work as a whole. For, while it is virtually impossible to find a novel which is "purely" representative of any of the categories, it is possible to recognize those which belong predominantly in one or another of them. Thus, the task of excluding and including becomes, though by no means mechanical, at least much easier.

But such a pragmatic rationale does not really supply solutions to the problems of categorization and exclusion. Perhaps nothing can. Certainly Malcolm Cowley's decision to reject categories altogether so that he may convey the "general picture that, emerging from all these books, becomes their most impressive feature" solves nothing; it leads to an even more exaggerated exclusiveness based almost solely on the arbitrariness of taste. In order to answer as well as possible these, my own, objections, I have introduced this study of the ideological war novels with a long look at these which will not be considered, except peripherally, in the body of the discussion. These include the combat novels, the psychological novels, and those novels which, because of a tendency to propagandize or to oversimplify ideology qualify merely as pseudo-ideological. This may not be a completely satisfactory solution, but at any rate, a number of worthy (and unworthy) novels which otherwise would have been ignored are given some attention.

I am indebted to many friends and colleagues for counsel and encouragement, primarily among them, Russel Nye, John Yunck, Adrian Jaffe, and Gene Bluestein. Two novelists deserve a vote of thanks as well, Anton Myrer and Prudencio de Pereda.

I am indebted too to the University College of Michigan State University for awarding the manuscript a University College Book Award; to the University itself for an All-University Research Grant; and to the College of Arts and Letters for a Research Professorship which gave me the time necessary to prepare this manuscript for publication.

A portion of this book appeared in *Wisconsin Studies in Contemporary Literature*. I wish to thank the editors for permission to reprint it.

The gist of much that follows appeared in an article of mine in *The Nation*, November 1, 1958. I wish to thank them for permission to use it here.

JOSEPH J. WALDMEIR
East Lansing, Michigan
September, 1966

CONTENTS

INTRODUCTION

Most of the war novelists write very knowingly about things concerned with war, from the progress of a platoon moving toward
its objective during the first few hours of an invasion (*A Walk
in the Sun*) to the progress of a total campaign on a Pacific island
(*The Naked and the Dead, The Thin Red Line*). They can take
an M1 apart in print by the numbers, or show, as John Hersey
does in *The War Lover*, how every gun aboard a B-17F operates.
They are especially adept at reporting, almost recording, the
speech of servicemen, from its monotonous obscenity through its
cluttered inarticulateness. It is generally agreed that the influence
of Hemingway is evident here. Doubtless it is; but one wonders
whether the novels might not have been equally detailed without
the example of *A Farewell to Arms,* whether the novelists might
not have decided independently that the most efficient way of
communicating the emotions attendant upon combat to the reader
is to present him with as objective and complete a portrait as
possible of the ground upon which the action takes place. Even
without Hemingway, it is likely that verisimilitude would be the
war novelist's intent and detailed completeness his means of
achieving it.

But if verisimilitude is an end in itself, if the novelist, as
William Dean Howells put it in a warning to the realist "heaps
up facts merely, and maps life instead of picturing it", the result
can be at best journalistic documentary and at worst artistic
disaster. All of the combat novelists flirt with this danger; it is
inherent in the category. Few of them escape completely un-
scathed. Those who make it do so largely because they are

quite selective, willing to limit their stories to brief segments of combat action and let these stand for the whole. Those who do not make it fail because they over-extend themselves trying to give the totality of a campaign, and the reader, instead of being impressed by the wealth and repetitiveness of the details, is overwhelmed and often bored by them. Harry Brown's *A Walk in the Sun* and Lawrence's Kahn's *Able One Four* are two of the most successful novels of combat; James Jones' *The Thin Red Line* is the category's most ambitious failure.

A Walk in the Sun is the story of the landing of an infantry platoon during the invasion of Italy, and of the platoon's movement toward the securing of their objective, a farm house six miles inland. The platoon is a veteran of the African and Sicilian campaigns. Its one inexperienced man, Lieutenant Rand, is killed while still on the landing barge, and the role of platoon leader falls to Sgt. Porter, whose nerves are beginning to give way. The platoon moves out, getting directions from a pair of Italian soldiers who are wandering aimlessly toward the beach in an effort to surrender. Combat experience pays off for the platoon as they ambush and destroy a German armored car; but the action sends Porter into combat fatigue. The platoon leaves him behind to wait for the medics, and proceeds under the command of Sgt. Ward. Upon reaching the objective, Ward leads a patrol to cover the opposite side of the house and is cut down by German enfilading fire. The platoon continues under the command of Corporal Tyne, and the story ends as he leads the attack on the farmhouse across an open field in the face of the machine gun fire that had killed Ward.

The story is nearly as matter-of-factly presented as this plot summary has been. Brown is interested primarily in the presentation of action; his message, if it can be so called, is simply that, given an experienced group of fighting men, any objective can be achieved despite minor impediments like armored cars and possible catastrophes like loss of leadership. He is not propagandizing for the American soldier and his "will to win"; there are no heroes in the novel. He is simply telling cleanly a truthful story. This is the principal reason that the book is so short (137 pages), as it is the reason that *Able One Four* (107 pages) is also short. Plotting and characterization need not be highly complex if the action is inherently dramatic and if there is no grand message or moral involved, or if the author is concerned only with immediate causes and their effects.

Sgt. Porter's breakdown is a case in point. Another author – Norman Mailer, for example – might have stopped the action in order to examine closely Porter's emotions and psyche, might even have dug into his pre-war background seeking by a sort of inverse prophecy to explain his collapse. Brown simply portrays his nervousness and his indecisiveness, then lets the attack on the armored car push him over the edge.

This is not to say that the combat adventure novelist cannot and does not look into the minds of his characters, permitting them to express attitudes and opinions, and to comment on their own mental and emotional conditions. Brown reports the thoughts both of Corp. Tyne and Sgt. Ward, permitting Ward to discover, just before his death, that:

The funny thing was that they were not very much concerned with what was facing them ahead. Each had his own problems, his own desires and wishes. They kept these personal things uppermost in their minds, as they had always done ever since they came into the Army. The war was incidental to a man's thoughts. It entered into them, of course, but it did not take them over bodily. There had been too many years of life, too many memories, before the war had come along. A man could exist on these memories, he could withdraw into them, he could construct them into an unpierceable shell. They were his defence against the violence of the world. Every man in the platoon had his own thoughts as he walked along, and they hovered unseen over the little group, an indefinable armor, a protection against fate, an indestructible essence.[1]

But Ward's discovery makes no difference. It has no effect on the outcome of the story; it has no measurable effect on the feelings or attitudes of the reader concerning the story.

Able One Four is told totally from the points of view of a five-member Tank Destroyer crew advancing with the infantry into Germany. We see the action entirely through the eyes of

[1] Harry Brown, *A Walk in the Sun*, p. 108.

Sgt. Tosky, a strong man and a good leader; Rick, a very green replacement; Dopey, a nice guy; Hungry, a somewhat cowardly goldbrick; and Spec, a brave man on the verge of a collapse like Porter's. Kahn, unlike Brown, even lets the reader witness Spec's paranoic nightmare in which he tries to cross quicksand to reach his wife who is plaintively calling his name from the other side of the bog. And too, we are a party to his waking thoughts:

Day after day you went through the motions of fighting a war. You lay around in basements or in the destroyer, you fired the gun or the machine guns at shadowy men who were always in front of you, you killed these men, but there were more, always more. They killed your friends, but there were more of these, too, and it went on and on. It would end when they killed him. It took too long. He was tired. He stared down the road, waiting for the men who would come to kill him, he had the tommy gun in his hands so he could kill them first, and he waited the long hours through till they came or till it was time for Rick to come up and wait.[2]

In the final analysis, the emphasis in both these novels remains unmistakably and satisfyingly on the combat action. The authors' interest in their characters' thoughts and feelings is subservient to their desire to portray briefly and concisely a combat situation. Thus, the walk in the sun is toward, and only toward, the climactic skirmish at the farmhouse; and thus the advance into Germany by the tank destroyer climaxes with the appearance of two Tiger tanks which demolish Tosky's gun, kill Rick, wound Hungry and Dopey, and push Spec over the edge beside Porter. None of the mental and emotional crises, nor any of the why we fight talk (there is a minimum of this, but for the most part, it is in the tone of the two quotations from the novels cited above), means anything outside the light of the fact of combat. These are simply not reflective novels; they are novels of action.

So is *The Thin Red Line,* but unfortunately it is far too long, and too unnecessarily involved, to sustain interest. It traces the actions of a total infantry company, including officers, enlisted men, and replacements through the Guadalcanal campaign. We meet each member of the company, however briefly, and we are

---

[2]   Lawrence Kahn, *Able One Four,* pp. 56-57.

treated to some excellent descriptions of combat action. But we are submerged, inundated by people and events. Unlike Brown and Kahn, Jones "heaps up facts merely", and the result is, as Howells warned it would be, a map rather than a picture of life – a map from which we feel more than once removed, as we felt when we saw the battle maps on the front pages of our newspapers during the war, with their arrows and dotted lines.

Norman Mailer calls *The Thin Red Line* "so broad and true a portrait of combat that it could be used as a textbook at the Infantry School if the Army is any less chicken than it used to be". He goes on to point out that "Jones' aim, after all, is not to create character but the feel of combat", by way of explaining the one-dimensional flatness of Jones' characters. And he concludes his very kind remarks by saying what must be said, that the novel is "too technical. . . . War is as full of handbooks as engineering, but it is more of a mystery, and the mystery is what separates the great war novels from the good ones." [3]

But it is not only the handbookishness or the refusal or inability to round out his characters which weakens Jones' novel, it is also his inability to write well. Mailer says (one suspects out of friendship) that "the faults and barbarities of his style are gone"; and one wonders how far he read into the book. On the very first page, two transports appear "in the first graying flush of dawn"; aboard them are some troops for whom "this was . . . to be their baptism of fire". And "the view which presented itself to them from the deck was a beautiful one". These are hardly isolated instances. The novel is crammed with cliches, redundancies, awkward constructions, and just bad writing. Whatever impact it retains despite its cumbersomeness is blunted by inept style.

All three of these novels are concerned to a certain extent with war as a traumatic experience. Porter and Spec both break under the constant pressure of combat; and 1st Sgt. Welsh, paranoic to begin with, by the end of *The Thin Red Line* has come to know "the combat numbness . . . and it was his calculated hope and belief that if pursued long enough and often

[3] Norman Mailer, *Cannibals and Christians*, pp. 112-13.

enough, it might really become a permanent and mercifully blissful state. It was all he asked".[4] But the primary emphasis of these novels is on combat, its feel and its effects; and the psychological difficulties of these characters is presented as simply one of the expected effects.

Some of the most interesting novels to come out of the war, however, are concerned *primarily* with war as traumatic experience, with the development and effects of war neurosis usually aggravated by the problems of youthful self-consciousness. Combat action underlies the novelists' concern here as a necessary cause, so too does ideology, if and when it appears at all. The novelists tend to agonize, often embarrassingly, over the painful psychological reactions of their characters to war, romanticizing, sometimes sentimentalizing their desperation. Even the three novels chosen to represent the category here – Vance Bourjaily's *The End of My Life,* William Hoffman's *The Trumpet Unblown,* and Prudencio de Pereda's *All the Girls We Loved* – do not escape completely, though by and large they are subdued, and as objectively written as their subjective subject matter will permit. In fact, all three are very well written, an advantage enjoyed by all too few of the war novels of whatever category.

Speaking of *The End of My Life,* John W. Aldridge says that "No book since *This Side of Paradise* has caught so well the flavor of youth in wartime, and no book since *A Farewell to Arms* has contained so complete a record of the loss of that youth in war. Actually, Bourjaily has written the one-volume, contemporary equivalent of both." [5] This is high praise indeed, though far too extravagantly enthusiastic. *The End of My Life* is a very good novel, but it is hardly good enough to stand up under the weight of comparison to Hemingway and Fitzgerald.

It is the story of Skinner Galt and three friends, Rod, Freak, and Benny, who join the British army in Africa as ambulance drivers. Their object in joining is twofold: to find adventure and to reject responsibility. " 'I want to see this war, just out of curiosity, and to say I've been' ", Skinner says to his college

[4] James Jones, *The Thin Red Line,* p. 445.
[5] John W. Aldridge, *After the Lost Generation,* p. 121.

roommate just before he enlists. He gestures at their room, adding, " 'I'd like to get all this crap out of my system.' " " 'Skinner Galt in search of reality, huh?' " the roommate asks, and Skinner answers, " 'Skinner Galt in search of a nice, thorough escape.' " [6]

But responsibility, both individual and social, is not to be denied. Freak comes to feel that his function as ambulance driver is worthwhile in humanitarian terms. Rod, in an attempt to rise above latent homosexual tendencies which soldier life has encouraged, deserts, like a latter day St. Anthony, seeking salvation among the Arabs in the desert. Benny discovers that he believes in the war even more strongly than Freak, strongly enough in fact to request transfer to the infantry. " 'No human being is an exception to humanity, Skinner' ", he says as he breaks the news of his transfer. " 'And this ambulance deal is an attempt to perpetuate the legend of non-participation. It lets you feel that you have chosen to try war, for the laughs, that you're at war voluntarily. I'm sick of feeling that way, Skinner. Maybe the infantry will knock it out of me." [7]

Freak has something to hold to, Rod something to run from, Benny something to run to. Only Skinner has nothing. " 'I don't think I want it knocked out of me', he replies to Benny. "I think it's the only thing that keeps me alive." [8] But Skinner is wrong. His attempt to hold onto the past through a continuing rejection of convictions and beliefs amounts actually to a rejection of life itself, and his mind rebels. He is subject to attacks of acute depression during which he retreats utterly into himself, performing his duties mechanically, almost completely out of connection with the world around him. The attacks

turned life into a sort of long endurance swim. You took a lot of deep breaths and paddled along the surface, in the sunlight for as long as you could. Then you began to tire, and you lost breath and began to sink, and at first you resisted sinking, but gradually the fight went out of you. And you floated down into the dark, cold depths, where the sun could no longer reach you.[9]

[6] Vance Bourjaily, *The End of My Life*, pp. 91-92.
[7] *Ibid.*, p. 212.
[8] *Ibid.*
[9] *Ibid.*, p. 198.

While in the deeps of one attack, he writes paranoic poetry: "Consider / The feeling of death / Inherent in the body / My body, your body, all bodies. / Built in." [10] And he thinks of suicide as "an intellectual position, the inevitable result of thinking things through to the end".[11]

But he always rises out of the depths, through the hangover of listlessness, to float buoyantly upon the cynical surface of life once again. Always, that is, until war itself takes a hand in investing him with a sense of responsibility. He has a brief affair with an army nurse, to whom he has communicated his own careless attitude toward life, and on a dare, they borrow a jeep and drive close to front line action. A German plane spots the vehicle and strafes it, killing the nurse instantly. Skinner ends in prison, with a year's sentence and dishonorable discharge before him.

The accident has a much more far-reaching effect on Skinner than the jail term or the discharge, however. For the first time in the novel, he truly feels his responsibility toward another human being. His affair with Johnny, the girl, had been simple and uncomplicated; he had not loved her. But this fact only compounds his sense of guilt – he had not cared, and not caring, he had acted stupidly, and his stupidity had led to tragic destruction. He plunges again into depression, but this time he knows it is too deep for him. He may rise out of it, but never into cynicism and irresponsibility again. And even more importantly, he does not want to become his old self once more. " 'I'm becoming dead' ", he says, rejecting his old friends, including the girl whom, as a civilian, he had promised to marry.

'Identity is a funny thing, and I'm losing it. Skinner Galt is on the way out. He had his day, now he's going. When I get out of here, I'll be someone else. Poor Mad Galt, perhaps, or Sailor Galt, or Virgil Galt, or even Galt the Ripper. But I'll be Tom Galt. I'm sure of that. I'm sick of Skinner. He's too God damn clever, and he hurt a lot of people.' [12]

[10]   *Ibid.*, p. 192.
[11]   *Ibid.*, p. 195.
[12]   *Ibid.*, p. 242.

He returns to his cell to await impatiently the listlesness out of which he will not emerge until the metamorphosis from Skinner to Tom is complete.

Eisinger includes *The End of My Life* within his Patterns of Despair category. He groups Bourjaily with those war novelists concerned with "violated sensibility", with those who "see only a confirmation of the cynicism which they had cultivated as the indispensable condition of their seeing at all".[13] But the novel, for all its grimness, is actually optimistic. War experience has not done as much *to* Skinner Galt as it has done *for* him. He had fought the discovery of himself, and this had been the major cause of his psychological upheaval. But war has forced him to face himself, as Freak and Rod and Benny had been forced to do, and now, finally, he himself is about to change. His traumatic experience has been a good thing; the war, if anything, has made him potentially a better man.

Tyree Shelby (*The Trumpet Unblown*) and Al Figueira (*All the Girls We Loved*) actually would fit Eisinger's pattern more conclusively than Skinner Galt, though hardly as cynics who entered the war with no illusions. They also are drastically changed by their war experiences, but in a quite different way from Skinner, and with quite different results. Because Skinner was selfish and irresponsible from the outset, there is a possibility that he may improve, may rise from his own ashes once his war-inspired psychological troubles have destroyed him. But Shelby and Al enter the war far more aware of their human responsibities than Skinner. Shelby volunteers as soon as he is old enough to be accepted into the army because it is in the tradition of his old Virginia family to fight America's wars, and because it is right to do so. Al pastes the following quotation from Lenin to his footlocker top:

Man's dearest possession is life, and since it is given him to live but once, he must so live as not to be seared with the shame of a cowardly and trivial past, so live as not to be tortured for years without purpose, so live that dying he can say: 'All my life and my strength were given to the first cause in the world – the liberation of mankind.' [14]

[13]   Chester E. Eisinger, *Fiction of the Forties*, p. 28.
[14]   Prudencio de Pereda, *All the Girls We Loved*, p. 9.

War-born psychological difficulties destroy Shelby and Al utterly. While Skinner sits in his cell awaiting the listlessness hangover out of which Tom Galt will be born, Shelby sinks deeper
and deeper into a depression out of which it seems he can never
rise, and Al puts a bullet in his brain.

Shelby, a medical corpsman, is assigned to a veteran Field
Hospital unit in England, awaiting the invasion of France. The
unit is made up primarily of Kentuckians [15] who had been through
the African and Sicilian campaigns; who, while not participants
in combat, had been witness to the tremendous carnage of combat; and who have reacted not with fear and humility but with
sadistic viciousness. It is as if the blood and gore have so jaded
their appetites, as if evil has become so attractive to them, that
they get no pleasure except in violence. The officers have long
since lost control of the men. In the first place, they are doctors
and nurses incapable of command except in pursuit of their
duties; in the second place, they are as morally corrupt, and for
much the same reason, as are the men. Captain Coger, neither
a doctor nor a medic, is the company commander of the enlisted
men. He is fundamentally a good man, but, caught between the
corruption of both his superiors and his charges, he has gradually
compromised his ability to command practically out of existence.
By the time Shelby joins the unit it is actually commanded by
two enlisted men: a drunken brute named Blizzard, and a physically, mentally, an economically powerful law unto himself named
Petras.

Blizzard rates the men according to toughness, forcing them
to fight among themselves under penalty of fighting him if they
refuse. Shelby refuses, and every night for a month he is pum-
meled by Blizzard, until finally, suspecting Shelby of having
reported him to Coger, Blizzard beats him badly enough to send
him to the hospital. Coger takes positive action and court martials
Blizzard, but he can only give him company punishment since

[15] Hoffman uses this symbolically, placing Shelby, the civilized representative of the Old Dominion who has volunteered as a gentleman to fight
in his country's cause among the savage representatives of the Frontier,
brawling brutes, fighting for the sake of fighting, not only un-realistic but
anti-idealistic.

the men are too frightened to testify against him. For the balance of the novel, Blizzard remains a physical threat to Shelby, taunting him, grinningly promising retribution.

But retribution is postponed by the invasion of France. Significantly, once the unit goes into operation, near harmony prevails. Although there is a great deal of drinking, as long as the wounded, the bleeding and the dying are being brought in, there is no carousing or mayhem. An air of sullen satisfaction settles around the unit, and it operates with supreme efficiency. Only Shelby, two other new men, Kemper and Silver, and Moody, Shelby's highly intelligent and sensitive tent mate are disturbed by the carnage. Moody begins drinking very heavily. The other three, with Petras' help, desert the unit and try to join the fighting troops. But as they cross a bridge under fire by 88's, Silver is killed and Shelby is thrown into shock. Only Kemper goes on. Shelby is returned to the hospital, incapable now even of escaping carnage by plunging into it.

Faced with what he interprets as his own cowardice, with the corrupt viciousness of the men and women of the hospital, and with the horrors of war in the person of the torn and mutilated wounded who pour in each day, Shelby gradually slips into depression. His world repels him, but there is no escape from it so he grasps a sense of duty, and begins his own destruction. He cannot escape, as Moody does, into alcoholism; nor can he adjust in Moody's terms: " 'You got to learn to think in terms of simple things. Think of beer. Think of sleep or the way a cigarette tastes. You got to learn to think of things isolated. That's what survival is. Think of sunshine.' " [16] His sense of right and wrong, of good and evil are too strong. He cannot stay and he cannot go and he cannot turn away. Like a robot, he works tirelessly among the wounded, and finally, among the tortured bodies newly freed from concentration camps. He is isolated, cut off from the world around him by repulsion for it, and cut off from the innocence that caused the repulsion by the evil surrounding him.

And symbolically, the unit too is isolated. At the war's end,

[16] William Hoffman, *The Trumpet Unblown*, p. 166.

they are sent to bivouac in a large, boggy meadow in the heart of Germany. Gradually, the troops around them move out, until finally, after many weeks, they are completely alone, apparently forgotten or consigned to a sort of Limbo. There is no hospital work to do. They are ordered to build a road through the area, and each day they dig and haul gravel, and each night the road disappears, sinking irretrievably into the bog. Inevitably, the sadistic violence begins again. Blizzard's pack runs once more; beatings and knifings are commonplace, but now the situation is much worse than it had been in England. The hospital chaplain who had exhorted the men to reform is discovered consorting with a farm girl in a field, and is driven trouserless to suicide under the wheels of a train. Petras designates himself commandant of a nearby village as yet untouched by Allied troops, and governs it for his own profit. The nurses and doctors gradually desert the unit, finding their ways presumably to other hospitals for reassignment until the well-meaning but impotent Captain Coger is the only officer left.

Petras takes Shelby under his wing, offering him his own survival of the fittest philosophy as the only viable one in the circumstances. And when Blizzard provokes Shelby into the long-awaited showdown by defiling a picture of his girl, Petras intervenes, precipitating a Jack London-like struggle between civilized and uncivilized brute force. Petras wins, breaking both of Blizzard's wrists and destroying his manhood with a deliberate kick. Then he deserts, as he necessarily must, leaving Shelby only the advice: "'Aim to survive. That's the whole secret.'"[17]

But for Shelby, survival is hardly simple. He's neither a Blizzard nor a Petras, but someone in between, someone whose honor and principles and illusions have all been either dirtied or destroyed by both friend and enemy, leaving him to nurse an unassignable guilt within his own bosom. It remains now only for him to contribute wilfully to his own destruction, to punish his world by punishing himself. He postpones the inevitable reckoning by clinging to the now acutely alcoholic Moody, trading regularly in the black market to keep him supplied with

[17] *Ibid.*, p. 211.

drink. On one of these errands, he is seduced by a German whore for stolen penicillin, and loses himself for three days in complete debauchery. When he returns to the unit, he finds that Moody in desperation had drunk wood alcohol and died a tortured, lonely death. Moody's death brings the unit to the attention of authority, and, rescued from their Limbo, the men are placed on rotation lists to be sent home.

The shock of Moody's death is too much for Shelby. Ridden by guilt, scarred by gonorrhea, the tangible symbol of his guilt, faced with the prospect of eventually going home and bearing with him his sin, his guilt, and his scar, he breaks down completely. At the novel's end, he is under psychiatric care, and has been furloughed against his wishes for thirty days. Adjustment seems impossible. His father still believes in honor and justice, but Shelby has been the victim of the pack; his girl is still prim and pretty, but first Blizzard then a German whore had defiled her. They no longer have a common ground; there is nothing they can even talk about. The fog of melancholy settles around him, even more thickly, and in the final scene of the novel he can only gaze at the darkened sky above his parents' brightly lit house, thinking hopelessly that "it was a long, a very long way to the stars".[18]

Guilt, growing out of a strong sense of responsibility, plays an important part in Al Figueira's mental difficulties too. However, Al's guilt is not precipitated or abetted by hatred of his own comrades as Shelby's is, but by love of them. And his is a rational, not an emotional or borrowed sense of responsibility. Shelby entered the war to fulfill tradition and because of a vague feeling that it was "right" to do so. Al entered it because of a firm belief in its justice and necessity.

Al is an ideological anti-Fascist who, along with Sidney Markowitz, his college friend, had tried to join the Loyalists in Spain. He was rejected for physical reasons, but Sidney went and was

---

[18] *Ibid.*, p. 256. *Yancey's War*, Hoffman's second war novel, presents the same sense of human folly and animal viciousness as *The Trumpet Unblown*; but here, the degradation and despair are softened by humor, by an absurdity of character and incident. Still, for all its comedy, *Yancey's War* is no less serious a treatment of men at war.

killed. Feeling himself at least partly responsible for Sidney's death, feeling more than a little guilty that he too has not died, and feeling as well that Sidney's death should not have been in vain – that the defeat of Fascism is a worthy cause to die in – Al eventually convinces the United States Army to take him, although he had been turned down twice as 4F. He is placed in ASTP to be trained for Intelligence service, and for a time, it seems that his guilty feelings are to be existed. He forms very close relationships with his fellow soldiers, particularly those with problems; he becomes a sort of father confessor for them:

'Every one of them had a problem. Maybe, it was because I had a problem myself, but I always seemed to hit that kind of guy and like them – and I got all their problems! Crazy happenings on furloughs, guys losing their girls, a guy who didn't have a friend in the world. . . .' [19]

Primarily because of the nature of the confessions, Al comes to the conclusion that not every soldier " 'is a rip-roaring antifascist. It's not so. Most of the guys are in because they were drafted, and most of them are fighting to win to get home – a kind of negotiated peace would be okay with most of them, I think.' " [20] And again: " 'you've got to work awfully hard to undo a lifetime of thinking. The guys just want to get home and get back to peace – the wife, the home, the baby and the job. . . . You still have to have other guys to spark them. I think I'm one of those guys.' " [21] Therefore, Al works a transfer to the infantry, to stand as an example, to lead the way, and " 'because I should have done it with Sid' " [22]

This rather complex set of motivations – guilt for Sidney Markowitz' death, a strong feeling of brotherhood for his fellow soldiers, a sense of responsibility for the cause behind the war – is further complicated when Al forms an extremely close friendship with Madison and Bernetto, two men with him in the same combat outfit. It is as if Sidney and all the soldiers he had known

[19]   *All the Girls We Loved*, p. 116.
[20]   *Ibid.*, p. 97.
[21]   *Ibid.*
[22]   *Ibid.*, p. 98.

and, for that matter, the whole human race has become symbolized by these two men. Al twines his life with theirs, satisfying his sense of responsibility and his desire for expiation. Madison and Bernetto become, in effect, a reason for living, and a reason for dying.

But during an assault in Germany, Madison and Bernetto are killed. And during the same assault, Al distinguishes himself sufficiently to earn the Congressional Medal of Honor. The medal is the crowning blow. It is bad enough that Madison and Bernetto, and Sidney, have been killed, it is bad enough that the cause has demanded sacrifice, but that he should at the same time be honored is too preposterous. Al retreats into a depression similar to Skinner's and Shelby's; and like Shelby, he finds himself under psychiatric care.

The main symptom of Al's psychological problems is impotence, or, as he terms it, "sexual sluggishness". It combines quite naturally with his inability to readjust to civilian life. He has no feelings for the woman he married shortly before he entered the army; he has no desire either to continue his studies at the university or to get a job. Al fears that his love for Madison and Bernetto had actually been homosexual; but the psychiatrist decides otherwise, and advises Al simply to find something else to fix his attention on, to find someone else to love. And Al finds Maya, a young, wealthy, beautiful, very desirable woman.

Slowly, Al's impotence abates as the idea occurs to him that he can alleviate his guilt by seducing Maya, that the seduction will be for Madison and Bernetto through him, that he can lay them finally to rest by offering the seduction up as a sort of expiatory sacrifice. The idea eventually becomes a conviction, then a monomaniacal fixation which gathers strength as fear of failure causes Al to postpone action.

Finally, he acts, after his wife has accused him of having acted already. He dons his uniform and waits outside Maya's apartment half the night, building his courage, facing himself, assuring himself, until finally, Maya returns from an evening out, and the impotence has fled. Al accosts her, frightened, like a nervous boy. When she rebuffs him, he shrivels up again, more hopelessly than ever. He strikes her, and returns to his own apartment. He puts on his dog tags, exchanges his shirt for one of Madison's which he has kept, and, while the telephone rings, he shoots himself to death with Bernetto's souvenir Luger.

Thus, Al Figueira, like Tyree Shelby, is destroyed, though for far different reasons. Thus too, Al and Shelby resemble Skinner Galt, though Skinner's fate is very different from theirs, since his destruction promises to result in a better man. But behind the complexities of love and hate, pessimism and optimism, hope and despair in all three novels looms the specter of war as cause or partial cause of the psychological problems of their heroes. It is war which brings Skinner Galt to face himself; it is war which places Shelby in the forsaken charnel house which is the field hospital; it is war that forces Al Figueira at the last to pull the Luger's trigger. And, in the combat novels, it is war which drives Spec and Porter over the edge and feeds Welsh's paranoia.

But not all men who went to war were affected similarly. The majority adjusted in one way or another, and simply rode the tide; and when the fighting ended, whatever psychological scars they had accumulated healed over rather quickly. And there was yet another group at the opposite pole from Skinner Galt and Tyree Shelby and Al Figueira who thrived on the danger of battle, on the killing and the threat of death, who found war stimulating, even sexually exciting. Characters like this appear in many of the war novels. Sgt. Croft in *The Naked and the Dead* is one, so is Pvt. Bell in *The Thin Red Line*; but the only full-length portrait of such a man is painted by John Hersey in *The War Lover*.

The portrait of Buzz Marrow is not as distinct as it might be because Hersey does not take us inside him, but rather reveals him to us through the points of view of his other principal characters. But what is revealed is clear enough. Buzz Marrow lives for war; he has no existence outside war. The tremors of his bomber as the bombs drop from it or as its guns begin to fire signal an orgasm in him; without violence he is impotent: " 'He can't make love' ", Daphne, the major female character says, " 'because love has to do with birth, life. When he gets in bed, he makes hate – attacks, rapes, milks his gland; and thinks that makes him a man.' " [23] And Charles Boman, Marrow's co-pilot and the narrator of the novel, comes to consider Marrow "my enemy, just as surely as the Nazis were. . . . He was a destroyer. He was in love with war. I could have no peace – the world could have none – if men like him were indulged in their passion." [24] Daphne echoes this fear and at the same time inadvertently points up the difference between the two kinds of psychological war novels:

'I think we ought to worry less about the future life, in peacetime, of the ones who break down in battle, and more about what's going to come of those who enjoy it too much. They're going to inflict their curse on the rest of us in peacetime. . . . Knives, billies, all that . . . They're going to pass it on to their children. We'll have other wars. . . .' [25]

However, as these passages indicate, *The War Lover* is not only a psychological study; Hersey is also concerned with why the war was fought, with why it had to be won and what might happen if it were lost – in short, with ideology. Boman doubts that a high and pure seriousness motivates his fellow soldiers. He sees each of them as either Buzz Marrow's or believers "in *Time* and the *Post* and *Colliers* and *Life*". And then a character named Lynch tells him why he fights:

'. . . it strikes me that in this century something awful has been let loose among the so-called civilized peoples, something primitive and barbaric. I don't say the Germans have a monopoly on this . . . this regression. But I figure I'm here to help put down the Nazis because right at the moment they're the most dangerous representatives of this sort of throwback we're liable to. If I can do my part in keeping this worst side of mankind in hand, I'll be satisfied, whatever happens to me.' [26]

Boman is so deeply affected that he takes a long first step toward conversion to belief in the war.

But Hersey's concern with ideology is not paramount in this

[23] John Hersey, *The War Lover*, p. 387.
[24] *Ibid.*, p. 169.
[25] *Ibid.*, p. 382.
[26] *Ibid.*, p. 231.

novel; it subserves the portrayal of Marrow, the lover of war, another dangerous representative of the throwback, though hardly an ideological one. Similarly, the basic motivation of Al Figueira's actions is ideological; but de Pereda's concern is not with ideas, but with the fact that Al's social consciousness has become inner directed, and *All the Girls We Loved* is really a study of the results of such inner direction. Both novels may contain ideology; neither however, is by definition an ideological novel, however.

Clearly, this is the place for a definition.

"The growth of ideology is closely related to the accumulation of social pressures", Irving Howe wrote in *Politics and the Novel*. "It is when men no longer feel that they have adequate choices in their styles of life, when they conclude that there are no longer possibilities for honorable maneuver and compromise, when they decide that the time has come for 'ultimate' social loyalties and political decisions – it is then that ideology begins to flourish." [27] This statement serves admirably as a basis for definition. If the novelists examine seriously and at length the ideas and principles which precipitated the war; if they question certain of the values which motivated the actions of individual servicemen; if, upon concluding "that the time has come for 'ultimate' social loyalties and political decisions", they offer constructive social criticism, their novels may be labeled ideological.

But please note, the term 'ideological' as it is used here applies only to novelists who are not satisfied with pat answers, whose ideology, while ultimately conclusive, is not based on simple assumptions of right and wrong, black and white. Certain World War II novels were based on such assumptions. Their social criticism is frequently over-simplified if not sentimentalized, and their ideology – assumed and accepted rather than molded out of serious doubts and questions – is sometimes more correctly termed propaganda. Not all of them are equally guilty however, and it might be sensible, before entering the prolonged discussion of the ideological novels planned for the succeeding chapters, to examine a few of these pseudo-ideological novels, as we have

[27] Irving Howe, *Politics and the Novel*, p. 160.

certain of the combat and the psychological novels. Such an examination should be even more worthwhile in this case, since, aside from suggesting a rationale for the selection of certain novels for discussion to the exclusion of others, it will help to clarify the definition of that most important term, 'ideological'.

John Hersey's first war novel, *A Bell for Adano,* is easily the best of the pseudo-ideological novels. It is concerned with the rehabilitation of conquered Italians along democratic lines. The flag is not waved too often or too hard in it, but the fact that it is not waved is too heavily underscored. America, Hersey makes clear, for all her gruffness and occasional meanness has more than her share of Christian goodness and charity. Adano is a city in Italy whose bell had been melted down by the Fascists to make bullets. The bell comes to stand as a symbol for the pre-Fascist Italy; its replacement symbolizes the resurrection and restoration of the old Italy by America. The plot and the "gimmick" present many opportunities for sentimentalizing and propagandizing. To Hersey's credit, he does not take them all.

Elliot Arnold in *Tomorrow Will Sing,* takes most of them. This is a novel in which Italo-American relations are strained because of the natural mistrust of a conquered people for its conquerors, because of Fascist propaganda that Italians are persecuted in America, and because of an economic slump in farming. An American Air Corps sergeant of Italian descent resolves all of these problems in addition to curing Italians of their prejudices. He suggests and successfully puts into operation a sort of farm cooperative; he plays over loud speakers one of Mayor La Guardia's Sunday speeches to the Italian people, proving thus that there is no nationalistic intolerance in America; and when he is robbed of the cooperative's receipts by an unregenerate fascist ex-soldier, and is accused of the theft himself, a large number of converted Italian character witnesses leap to his defense. The novel ends on a high note: every American finally knows what he is fighting for.

Hersey and Arnold plot well and draw characters convincingly, so that, despite their over-simplification, *A Bell for Adano* and *Tomorrow Will Sing* convey an air of sincerity that almost compensates for their lack of depth. But within the general classification of propaganda novels there is a large sub-group which owe their reason for being to the oversimplification; they exist on the surface. These are the "gung-ho" combat novels. They embrace the naive ideological assumption that America is always right and always good, that therefore her causes are worth fighting for without question or argument, and that anyone, ally or enemy, who is not with her is definitely against her. There is a good deal of sentimentalized dying, heart-of-goldness-beneath-a-gruff-exterior, and poetic justice in them. Most of them came out early in the war, riding the wave of sentimental patriotism; but there have been some rather successful ones, like Leon Uris' *Battlecry* and James Jones' *From Here to Eternity,* since the war's end. Both appear to be seriously realistic and to have important ideological backgrounds, but both actually depend for most of their effectiveness on the "gung-ho" tradition.

In *Battlecry,* a wayward youth returns to and marries his pure first love, leaving the Scarlet Woman dripping tears into her martini. A meek, bespectacled (hence, sensitive) marine turns out to be every bit as tough as anyone else in his company; and, although he is killed, the whore he has converted to a straight and narrow path lives on, a pure testimonial to his enduring goodness. An embittered one-legged hero finds peace as the husband of an Australian war widow, upon the land and among the trees of her magnificent farm. Finally, and most importantly, the regimental commander's rugged training techniques, so roundly condemned by the men, are vindicated at Guadalcanal and Tarawa – the Japanese are driven back, pounded down, and soundly defeated, in the true "gung-ho" manner:

Huxley's Whores rose to the heights of their dead captain. They no longer resembled human beings. Savage beyond all savagery, murderous beyond murder, they shrieked, 'Blood!'
    'BLOOD!' . . . 'BLOOD!'
    The enemy, who were mere mortals, fell back.[28]

[28] Leon Uris, *Battlecry*, p. 498. A "gung-ho" novel is difficult to define except by such examples. One might make the point however, that it was the sort of war novel which, when made into a motion picture, starred William Bendix.

From Here to Eternity appears on the surface to be a much more serious book than *Battlecry*. In the first place, it contains a good deal of frank toughness. In the second place, the army, its officers and its men, are not idealized throughout the major portion of the book; in fact, Jones sometimes seems to be exposing all the pettiness and sadistic meanness of soldier life in the regular army. But he lapses completely into dependence on the "gung-ho" tradition for his denouement. With the attack on Pearl Harbor, differences, some of them murderous, among the soldiers disappear, become lost in the pursuit of a greater good: the defeat of an insidious foe. The army jells; there is a war to be won, and the men now have a purpose for existing. Jones' basic assumption seems to be that there is no such thing as a bad boy. Give a boy something to do, and he will work his way out of tendencies to whoring, homosexuality, alcoholism, and sadism. And he will perform valiantly during war because he is, above all else, an American.

Some of the novels must be labeled pseudo-ideological not because of an appeal to the sentimental nor because of a tendency toward the Gung-Ho pose, but because they are just badly thought out and wrought out. Such a one is Peter Bowman's blank verse novel, *Beach Red*, in which all of the action at the invasion of a Pacific island is seen through the eyes of one doomed soldier. His thoughts are muddled, perhaps understandably, by the tensions and pressures of his situation, and all of the muddiness is conveyed to the reader. He feels that he is fighting to avenge the Bataan death march: "Do unto Japs as Japs do unto you – but first." [29] He feels that the monument to war should be a drainage ditch

... with a pole over it and a crudely lettered sign saying "latrine". And all the Joes would come and urinate in it and empty their bowels in it and throw garbage in it and fill it with red liquid that looks like blood. And people would watch it flowing like a public fountain and they would smell it and they would be reminded of war.[30]

At another point, he feels that he is fighting for trees, grass a

[29] Peter Bowman, *Beach Red*, p. 78.
[30] *Ibid.*, p. 102.

car, a girl, hamburgers, movies, hot baths, gay neckties, trolley cars, and peanuts at a baseball game. And a moment later he insists that "Nobody stands up and strikes an attitude and says, 'This is what I'm fighting for.' " [31] War, he concludes shortly thereafter, is a duty of citizenship, for both Japanese and Americans; but ironically, "Battle doesn't determine who is right. Only who is left." [32]

But one is caught up in this hectic story of one soldier's last frantic hour on earth to the point where he tends to overlook its inconsistencies and unfortunate muddiness. It is much less easy to forgive the bad aspects of a novel such as Hobert Skidmore's *Valley of the Sky,* a book which might be considered the archetype of the pseudo-ideological propaganda novels.

This is an Air Corps story about a B24 crew fighting the war in the Pacific. The plane is named "The Heartless Harpie", and it and its crew "go through hell" fighting for Democracy and for the American Way. Individual members of the crew think about why they fight and die while they fight and die, and they kill in happy this-one's-for-my-buddy vengeance.

Blood was running down Kris' face and across the front of his dislodged mask.

Kris opened his eyes slightly, as if he had never opened them wider. "John, drive them into the water, blow them up", he whispered hoarsely and then his eyes closed. "Slaughter a generation", he pleaded.[33]

And as John prepares to avenge his dead buddy, he thinks

... progressing, unhurried thoughts that told him victory was near and yet beyond his time. He had known it since that afternoon on the road in Ohio. It had been his compulsion to enlist. Of course. That was it. He had almost known it all the time. They had forgotten what America meant and those who became alert quickest, fought quickest, sacrificed readily. It was as simple and right and inevitable as that, he realized. Men who know loyalty and belief and freedom, know death, too, for death, rightfully acquired, contains these.[34]

And shortly thereafter, having accomplished her mission, the plane is destroyed by two fighters (taking one of them with her,

[31]   *Ibid.,* p. 104.
[32]   *Ibid,.* p. 106.
[33]   Hobert Skidmore, *Valley of the Sky,* p. 160.
[34]   *Ibid.*

however). The crew dies gloriously, and "all men who ride on the wings of the heavens listen for the Harpie, knowing her spirit was infinite".[35] Brown, Bowman, Kahn and other fine combat-adventure novelists were aware that such sentimental romanticism is unrealistic under combat conditions, and either didn't employ it or, like Bowman, specifically disavowed it.

But there is yet a better example of Skidmore's desire to propagandize. Upon reaching its island base at the outset of the novel, the Harpie is surrounded by news-starved soldiers who pelt its crew with questions. One of the plane's new ground crewsmen, a father of two, inquires anxiously whether or not the allotment has been increased. " 'They're voting on it now. It's in Congress, I think' ", he is told. He hurries away to get his tools, for the Harpie must be readied for combat, and Skidmore writes:

Homer Harlan Miller, private and handyman, visualized the distant and high machinery of free government at work for him and for Mary and little Rose Ellen and for new boy, Homer Harlan. The whole government was thinking of him and those he loved and they were going to take care of them. His family would be secure now, until he returned, and for the first time in months tears ran down his cheeks as he prayed; the hot wells of gratitude and relief poured from his quiet eyes. His prayer was simple. 'Thank you, thank you, thank you', he repeated as he arranged each tool in an orderly row. It was hard for him and the thousands like him to love or to hate violently, and now that hatred of an enemy was constantly growing in him, love only came in infrequent and overwhelming waves, pouring itself out in gratitude for its own existence and with it now were all the unexpected wonders of free government, of men meeting in congress to help their fellow men. The relief was a glorious thing, shining about his eyes and he picked up his tools in his calloused hands and turned toward the mat. The giant ship rested there, her sides and wings bronzed by the sunset. He had never seen one look so dignified and purposeful. 'I'll help fix her up', he said to himself. 'I'll fix her up for Congress'.[36]

The quotation is long, but its very length helps to fix the point: This sort of writing is propaganda posing as ideology. The characters are stock, as are the reader responses. *Valley of the Sky*

---

[35] *Ibid.*, p. 169.
[36] *Ibid.*, p. 62.

was written at a time when it was possible to put an American into a GI uniform and make him therefore a right-thinking hero. Most of the pre-war anti-Nazi novels are guilty of the same over-simplifications for many of the same reasons. John Steinbeck in *The Moon Is Down*, for example, could put a character into a German uniform and make him automatically a villain; or could invent a collaborator and have the reader understand that he is therefore a coward; or could give a woman a bady and/or a dead husband and make her *per se* capable of magnificent heroism in her own right. The stock response is the stock in trade of such novels as *The Moon Is Down* and *Valley of the Sky*, and of the many "gung-ho" novels, most of which are much worse than *Battlecry* and *From Here to Eternity*. It is less the stock in trade of the slightly more serious pseudo-ideological novels like *A Bell for Adano* and *Tomorrow Will Sing*, but here too, the stock response has been too blandly appealed to and manipulated.

But the serious ideological novel is not a sentimentalized acceptance without question and propagation without discrimination of old cliches and tired truisms; nor is it simply a realistic account of combat action of psychological difficulties. It is an attempt to blend these ingredients artistically with firm ideological convictions into a conclusive ideological statement. The novelists are intent upon a re-examination and a re-evaluation of the fundamentals and bases of the American ideology, as well as of the ideology of the total Western world. The war, as a struggle with fascism, serves as a focal point for these fundamentals; the services as a vantage point from which to watch them in operation in an extraordinary situation. It is a situation sufficiently extraordinary to put the fundamentals to the supreme test, for the easily controlled controls, the conditioned responses of a peacetime or even, during wartime, a civilian America, are missing. The novels are complex entities, motivated by complex social, cultural, intellectual, and emotional forces. They contribute much more valuably to an understanding of the nation, its soldiers, and the war than do the combat adventure, the psychological, or the propaganda novels, and for these reasons they merit the extended attention to be paid them in the ensuing chapters.

I. NOVELISTS OF TWO WARS

Two points have consistently been made concerning the derivation of the World War II novels. The first is that, except for their stylistic debt to Hemingway, they are nothing like the World War I novels; the second is that they have been strongly influenced by the crusading social criticism of the 1930's. Both points must be dealt with here, not because they are inaccurate – indeed, they are quite true – but because they are most often made as charges, loaded with the contradictory implication that the novels are weaker for being at once too derivative and not derivative enough. A close examination of both points will accomplish two things: it will serve as a corrective to the implication, and, more importantly, it will establish the background out of which the ideological novel of the second War emerged.

The frequently repeated challenge to be shown the Hemingway and Dos Passos of the second war, simply because it is a challenge, can only be answered with: there are none. There is a Stefan Heym, a Norman Mailer, a John Horne Burns, an Irwin Shaw, an Alfred Hayes, a Joseph Heller – there is even a Herman Wouk and a James Gould Cozzens – but there is no Hemingway or Dos Passos, nor is there a William March, or a Thomas Boyd, or a Dalton Trumbo, or a Humphrey Cobb. Such an answer offers nothing which can clarify the relationship between the two groups of novelists; but it is the only answer possible given the nature of the challenge.

However, nothing could be more reasonable than an objective comparison of the two groups. After all, each war was fought in the same half century against the same enemy; each was the most vicious and deadly and all-embracing war up to its time. If the novelists who came out of each were so absolutely different, and if the novelists saw and portrayed their wars honestly, an examination of their differences would seem unquestionably to be in order.

The post-World War I generation of the 1920's, as Frederick Hoffman puts it in *The Twenties*:

... felt honestly that it had been victimized by a gross and stupid deception. Nothing genuine had come out of the war. American politicians had refused to accept their responsibility in a world league (which, as it was plotted at Versailles, seemed unworkable anyway) and had chosen isolation. The elders had made fools of themselves, and involved the young in murderous folly; how could they respect them? [1]

And again:

The failure of the war as they [the young] saw it was proof of the absurdity of the forces that had caused it and of the propaganda which had helped to bring it to a successful conclusion.[2]

This cynical disillusionment pervades the ideological novels of the first war. Its classis statement is made by Frederic Henry in *A Farewell to Arms*:

I was always embarrassed by the words sacred, glorious, and sacrifice and the expression in vain. We had heard them, sometimes standing in the rain out of earshot, so that only the shouted words came through, and had read them, on proclamations that were slapped up by billposters over other proclamations, now for a long time, and I had seen nothing sacred, and the things that were glorious had no glory and the sacrifices were like the stockyards at Chicago if nothing was done with the meat except to bury it. There were many words that you could not stand to hear and finally only the names of places had dignity. Certain numbers were the same way and certain dates and these with the names of the places were all you could say and have them mean anything. Abstract words such as glory, honor, courage, or hallow were obscene beside the concrete names of villages, the numbers of regiments and the dates. Gino was a patriot, so he

[1] Frederick Hoffman, *The Twenties*, p. 77.
[2] *Ibid.*, p. 78.

said things that separated us sometimes, but he was also a fine boy and I understood his being a patriot. He was born one.[3]

Such a relatively calm statement is rare in the World War I novels. John Andrews in Dos Passos' *Three Soldiers,* for instance, is not simply embarrassed by the ideals of duty and patriotism; he is angered by them. " 'Oh, those long Roman words, what millstones they are about men's necks!' " he cries, adding: " 'It seems to me ... that human society has been always ... and perhaps will be always ... organizations growing and stifling individuals, and individuals revolting hopelessly against them, and at fast forming new societies to crush the old societies and becoming slaves again in their turn.' " [4] Armies are such organizations, armies and governments which use the "long Roman words" as propaganda for the senseless barbarity of war. And churches too. In *Three Soldiers,* a Rev. Dr. Skinner bemoans the fact, before a congregation of wounded and crippled soldiers, that the Allies had not crushed Germany utterly – then he leads the singing of the hymn, "Stand Up, Stand Up for Jesus." [5]

William March, in *Company K,* castigates "Christian people who pray in their churches for the destruction of their enemies, and glorify the barbarity of their soldiers in bronze. . . . " [6] And, in one of the most bitterly ironic passages in all the war novels, March portrays the unknown-soldier-to-be, terribly wounded, trapped on the barbed wire of no-man's land. As he hangs there hoping for a quick death, it occurs to him that there will be prayers and patriotic speeches over his heroic corpse, and he cries out above his agony: " 'I can't stand the thought of that! I can't stand it! ... I never want to hear military music or high sounding words again: I want to be buried where nobody will ever find me – I want to be wiped out completely. . . . ' " Feverishly then he destroys all possibility of identifying his remains, and convinces a sympathetic German soldier that he should be put out of his misery. And he dies whispering: " 'I have broken

[3] Ernest Hemingway, *A Farewell to Arms,* p. 196.
[4] John Dos Passos, *Three Soldiers,* p. 458.
[5] *Ibid.,* pp. 233-34.
[6] William March, *Company K,* p. 178.

the chain. .... I have defeated the inherent stupidity of life.' " [7]

March, like Hemingway and Dos Passos, tended to take the catastrophe of the war personally, to see the blood and death, the stupidity and viciousness as degradations of the individual. And as a consequence, their bitter disillusionment is expressed in terms of the individual and the action which grows out of the disillusionment is performed by the individual in the name of the individual: March's Unknown Soldier breaks the chain by his anonymous suicide; Frederic Henry and John Andrews break it by their desertion. All three reject any responsibility to that society which can cause war to be perpetrated; none of the three is concerned, except by inference, with that portion of society equally victimized by the war. Angry, disillusioned, iconoclastic – they simply want out.

Such an attitude, not only toward war, but toward life generally, formed the ideological ground for much of the literature of the 1920's – though of course it was not confined to those years; *Company K* appeared in 1933. It was especially characteristic of that group of writers who allowed themselves to be called the "lost generation". Destructive rather than constructive in their social criticism, they asserted a belief only in "nada" – a belief not in nothing but in the reduction of something to nothing; a belief in the condemnation of everything "normal" on the ground, supported by the observable cause and effect of the war, that normality equates with invalidity. Their attention was focussed, logically enough, on the individual, the single irreducible unit in society, the only unit which can be relied upon to react at least partially predictably. The individual is neither an idea nor a movement; he is no larger than himself or his set of reactions, and he may therefore be gotten hold of, be seen entire – in relation to the forces controlling him certainly, but at the same time above or beyond those forces. He, whether he be Frederic Henry or John Andrews or a nameless member of an infrantry company, can speak for himself without regard, really, for Society or the People or Movements.

Ironically, 1929 vindicated completely this pessimistic icono-

[7] *Ibid.*, p. 123.

clasm, but resulted in one of the greatest periods of social optimism in American intellectual history. The 1930's belief in
positive action, in the justice of concrete causes, was not a reaction to pessimism but was a logical result of it. The iconoclasts
had been proved correct; now action was necessary. In like
manner, the 1920's anti-World War I writers stand in a cause
to effect relationship to the belligerent World War II novelists.
The second war was fought to protect the gains which had been
won as a result of the social struggles of the 1930's – struggles
which had been motivated largely by the bitter iconoclasm of
the 1920's. Within twenty years, the term 'liberal' as used by
Americans was successfully redefined so that it came very nearly
to mean the exact opposite of its old self. But even more amazing,
the redefinition was not a result of disenchantment with the old
definition; the new seemed indeed, necessarily to follow from
the old.

Mitigating this irony somewhat was the growth of a distinctly
social literature concurrently with the romantic liberal-individu-
alism of the 1920's. Fed by the liberal tradition of the 'teens,
and by the rise of the Soviet Union, writers such as Mike Gold
and Joseph Freeman, Max Eastman and Floyd Dell, in such
publications as *The Liberator* and *The New Masses,* worked
firmly to establish an ideological position almost counter to that
of the lost generation. For them, the social evil of normality
remained essentially the same, but the solution was engagement,
commitment, indignant affirmation rather than disillusioned negation, rather than nada. Their voices cried weakly in the wilderness
of the '20's, drowned out by the only sorts of social criticism
the decade would countenance – the japes and gibes of a
Mencken or the weak-tea satire of a Sinclair Lewis. But by the
1930's, the ideological ground they had prepared, fed by the
fear, the pain, the anger, and the hope of the Great Depression
was ready to produce a significant literature of social protest.[8]

The war novelists of the 1930's, represented here by the Dos

[8] See Walter Rideout, *The Radical Novel in the United States,* and Daniel
Aaron, *Writers on the Left* for comprehensive discussions of these shifting
ideological positions.

Passos of *1919*, by Humphrey Gobb and by Dalton Trumbo, reflect very well this ideological shift from iconoclastic liberalism to social protest. They hated World War I as passionately as had the writers of the '20's. They could understand and sympathize with the cynical bitterness of *A Farewell To Arms, Three Soldiers*, and *Company K*, but they could not in conscience subscribe to it; for they found that more than the individual had lost in the useless viciousness and cruelty – all mankind had lost. Their modification took the war novel into the mainstream of social realism and social consciousness. The prevention of such another catastrophe, they felt, demanded action, not rejection. It demanded that the issue be attacked rather than retreated from whether the retreat was to Switzerland with Catherine and the baby she carried inside her, or to a Parisian room with the strains of a symphony running through one's blood (both the child and the music must be stillborn anyway). It demanded that one make his death meaningful by identifying himself and thus accusing, rather than perishing in self-satisfactory anonymity.

Although *1919* is not a war novel in any absolute sense, it is concerned sufficiently with the war and the peace, with their causes and consequences, to belong in this discussion. Furthermore, it serves as a legitimate transition piece between the novels of the '20's and '30's, for the somewhat discursive bitterness of *Three Soldiers* is more controlled and specific in *1919*, within the framework of social criticism. The most pointed commentary comes in the historical-biographical vignettes, such as "The House of Morgan", in which Dos Passos argues that the war was fought to protect American financial interests abroad: "By 1917 the Allies had borrowed one billion, nine-hundred million dollars through the House of Morgan: we went overseas for democracy and the flag. . . . " [9] The vignette ends with the refrain:

> (Wars and panics on the stock exchange,
> machinegunfire and arson,
> bankruptcies, warloans,

[9]   Dos Passos, *1919*, p. 340.

starvation, lice, cholera and typhus:
good growing weather for the House of Morgan.) [10]

To describe the atmosphere in which the Versailles Treaty was written, in the vignette, "Meester Veelson" Dos Passos alters the refrain to read: "machine gun fire and arson /starvation, lice, cholera, typhus;/ oil was trumps." "On April 19", he continues:

> sharper Clemenceau and sharper Lloyd George got
> him [Wilson] into their cozy three card game
> they called the Council of Four.
> On June 28th the Treaty of Versailles was ready
> and Wilson had to go back home to explain to the
> politicians who'd been ganging up on him meanwhile
> in the Senate and the House and to sober public opinion
> and to his father's God how he'd let himself be trimmed
> and how far he'd made the world safe
> for democracy and the New Freedom.[11]

A third vignette, "The Body of an American", is concerned with the selection and ceremonious entombment of the Unknown Soldier. It is easily as bitter and angry as the selection from *Company K* cited above; it is even more realistically vicious in its detail: "The blood ran into the ground, the brains oozed out of the cracked skull and were licked up by the trenchrats, the belly swelled and raised a generation of bluebottle flies." [12] But Dos Passos has made the details serve, if not an openly social, at least a less personal purpose than March. There is no falling and bleeding upon the thorns of life here; no vainglorious attack upon "the inherent stupidity of life". From its opening injunction to the selectors of the fortunate corpse to "Make sure he ain't a dinge, boys,/ make sure he ain't a guinea or a kike",[13] to its bitterly ironic ending:

> and the incorruptible skeleton,
> and the scraps of dried viscera and skin bundled in
> khaki.
> they took to Chalons-sur-Marne

[10]   *Ibid.*
[11]   *Ibid.*, p. 249.
[12]   *Ibid.*, p. 472.
[13]   *Ibid.*, p. 468.

and laid it out neat in a pine coffin
and took it home to God's Country on a battleship
and buried it in a sarcophagus in the Memorial
Amphitheatre in the Arlington National Cemetery
and draped the Old Glory over it
and the bugler played taps
and Mr. Harding prayed to God and the diplomats
and the generals and the admirals and the brasshats
and the politicians and the handsomely dressed ladies out
of the society column of the Washington Post stood up
solemn
and thought how beautiful sad Old Glory God's Country
it was to have the bugler play taps and the three volleys
made their ears ring.

Where his chest ought to have been they pinned the
Congressional Medal, the D.S.C., the Medaille Militaire,
the Belgian Croix de Guerre, the Italian gold medal, the
Vitutea Militara sent by Queen Marie of Rumania, the
Czechoslovak war cross, the Virtuti Militari of the Poles,
a wreath sent by Hamilton Fish, Jr., of New York, and a
little wampum presented by a deputation of Arizona red-
skins in warpaint and feathers. All the Washingtonians
brought flowers.

Woodrow Wilson brought a bouquet of poppies.[14]

the vignette is infused with a social awareness which is absent
from the earlier war novels, including Dos Passos' own *Three
Soldiers*, and which profoundly deepens and expands its bitter
meaning.

Both Cobb and Trumbo emphasize the social theme even more
explicitly than Dos Passos. *Paths of Glory* is the story of the
arrest, trial, and execution of five French infantrymen for cowardice and mutiny. The men are not guilty; Cobb makes this
absolutely clear. A vainglorious General orders an attack on
German positions made impregnable by terrain and well-placed
machine-gun defenses. After its failure, in order to cover the
fact that the attack should never have been made in the first
place, the General orders that one man from each of five units
be selected for execution as an example to the rest. The men

14 *Ibid.*, pp. 472-73.

are chosen by lot – each of the five fought as well and as long as he could; none of them ran – given a token trial, and submitted to a firing squad.

Cobb places his story squarely in the realm of social criticism by showing, in a "Note" at the end of the text, that the book is based on fact. "All the characters, units, and places mentioned in this book are fictitious", he writes:

> However, if the reader asks, 'Did such things really happen?' the author answers, 'Yes', and refers to the following sources which suggested the story; *Les crimes des conseils de Guerre*, by R. G. Reau; *Les fusilles pour l'exemple*, by J. Gautier Roissiere and Daniel de Ferdon; *Les dessous de la guerre*, by Paul Allard; a special despatch to *The New York Times* of July 2, 1934, which appeared under this headline: 'FRENCH ACQUIT 5 SHOT MUTINY IN 1915; WIDOWS OF TWO WIN AWARDS OF 7 CENTS EACH'; and *Le fusille*, by Blanche Maupas, one of the widows who obtained exoneration of her husband's memory and who was awarded damages of one franc.[15]

But Cobb's social indignation is most apparent in his portrayal of the victims as little, almost anonymous men, men who stand no chance against a ruling class or order. "We have learned who our enemies are", wrote Charles Yale Harrison in *Generals Die in Bed* " – the lice, some of our officers, and death." *Paths of Glory* is a bitter echo of the statement.

The hero of *Johnny Got His Gun* is victimized by war itself rather than by forces, such as self-seeking officers, simply attendant upon war. He too is a little man, an American private

---

[15] Humphrey Cobb, "Note" to *Paths of Glory*, p. 265. The problem of mutiny plagued the French army for two years, reaching its apex during the spring and summer offensive of 1917. Faced with murderous German machinegun fire, a significant proportion of the *poilu* refused to attack. Some of them simply sat; some deserted, either to go to Paris for riotous flings, or to return to their homes. The mutiny lasted until General Robert Nivelle was replaced by General Henri Petain as commander of the infantry, whereupon the suicidal tactics changed, and the grievances of the soldiers concerning proper rest, competent medical service, and proper provisions for leave were at least partially rectified. A number of the mutineers was executed; no one knows how many since a cloak of secrecy has surrounded the incident all these years, and the French apparently offer little hope that it will soon be lifted. *Dare Call It Treason* by Richard M. Watts is the most complete and authoritative discussion of the 1917 affair yet published.

soldier who, as the result of a shell burst, has become a basket case. He has no arms nor legs, no stomach, no face. He suspects that he is truly anonymous to the people caring for him, though he cannot be certain – and he could do nothing about it in any case, since he cannot speak, hear, or see. Neither can he feel or taste. But he can remember, and Trumbo painstakingly portrays the psychological agony growing out of his memories of home and love coupled with his realization that he is now, irrevocably, as an inevitable result of war, a monster. At this point, Trumbo would have been justified in allowing Johnny the condition of romantic despair, the condition of March's unknown soldier; he comes close, for Johnny wishes and prays for death repeatedly throughout the novel. But finally, at the crucial moment, Johnny's social consciousness takes hold and he resolves to remain alive as a pacifist reminder and object lesson to his fellow man that only evil and agony can come of war.

Smouldering anger, crusading indignation, high optimism – along with a hyper-realistic, almost naturalistic, style – made the socio-ideological novel of the 1930's singularly convincing and persuasive. In the hands of a Dos Passos, a James T. Farrell, or a John Steinbeck it became also artistically singular. But there were traps built into the genre which caught many of the novelists, including Cobb and Trumbo, and seriously impaired the artistry of their books. Tyrannized by their subject matter and by their own seriousness, they often, quite unintentionally, turned their novels into tracts or sermons; their plots were ridden by the theme, and the characters, ridden by the plot, flattered out and became representational. And while the ideological import of the books was often thereby strengthened, their artistic effect was correspondingly weakened. The doomed characters in *Paths of Glory*, for example, gradually lose their human depth as they come more and more to represent ways to face injustice and death. Only Captain Etienne, their defender, possesses distinctly human characteristic – he can pity, or love, or hate – but Cobb shies away from the Captain's point of view and remains reporter, as if fearing that his message might get lost in the individual. And Trumbo's Johnny is not so much a human being as he is a pacifist argument. The situation is too abnormal; Johnny's thoughts and desires are too perfectly in tune with the book's message. This is evident when in page after page Johnny denounces his sacrifice as unnecessary, denies the validity of the war's causes, and wishes his fate upon all the perpetrators of war. But it is most evident at the novel's ending which, suspenseful and powerful though it is, supplies a perfect example of what can happen to the artistry of a novel if the writer tries too hard to make it argumentatively conclusive. Through exercise, Johnny strengthens his neck muscles until he can tap out Morse code messages with his head, and after many attempts, he gets someone to understand him. In an incredible scene, Johnny requests to be placed on display in the name of ideological pacifism; the novel ends as a curt refusal, in the name of patriotism and good taste, is tapped out on his forehead.

The ideological novelists of the second World War despised the animal-like living, killing, and dying of war as positively and thoroughly as had their World War I counterparts. Death, destruction, mayhem, maiming, the terrors of battle fatigue are portrayed in novel after novel in all their capriciousness. The brave, like Noah Ackerman in Irwin Shaw's *The Young Lions,* are killed; so are the honest, like Lt. Hearn in Norman Mailer's *The Naked and the Dead*; the good, like Sgt. Bing in Stefan Heym's *The Crusaders*; and the gifted, like Alan Newcombe in Anton Myrer's *The Big War*. No man can control his destiny, and there is no compensating glory in war to ease the pain of body or conscience. The "dramatic mood of well-here-we-go-again-off-to-the-wars" expressed by John Horne Burns in one of the first person "Promenades" in *The Gallery* is stifled rapidly by the stark reality of the moral and physical degeneration of people caught up in war. " 'Fighting a war to fix something works about as good as going to a whorehouse to get rid of a clap' ", says Red in *The Naked and the Dead*.[16] And "It's all wrong", says the doomed Danny Kantaylis of *The Big War* to his new wife, Andrea

16 Norman Mailer, *The Naked and the Dead*, p. 578.

'I don't see any way out of it, I don't see we've got any choice now
except go all the way, kill as many of them as we can – but it's all wrong,
just as wrong as when Jesus said it was. Or the Ten Commandments
either. And anything that makes a big, glorified deal out of killing is
rotten through: anything at all. It's a foul, dirty, cruddy business. . . .
And it's only right we're doing it in a lousy cruddy jungle, too. Perfectly fitting and proper. . . .' [17]

And – again similarly to the World War I novelists – with the
possible exception of Herman Wouk and James Gould Cozzens,
whose ideas will be discussed in a future chapter, the World
War II writers condemned the armed services and were harshly,
even bitterly, critical of many enlisted men and most officers.

Such evidence has led some critics to conclude that the novelists were not concerned with the meaning of the war at all.
John T. Fredericks charges them with "failures in vision, failure
to see in the horrible jungle of war the root and leaf of human
meaning. For too many of these writers, the surface of experience is enough, the surface is all." [18] And it has led others to
read the novels as if whatever meaning they do contain can be
interpreted only in terms of the lost generation yet more lost.
John W. Aldridge, for example, in *After the Lost Generation*
asserts that the war novelists "were able only to present the
gigantic zero of what they saw, for they never had the hope and
the essential faith they needed to make an effective protest". He
goes on to saddle them with an ideological disillusionment far
blacker and deeper than that of the World War I novelists:

The greatest failure . . . the thing that has left its stamp upon the weaknesses of all their novels, has been the failure in their time of a basic
belief in the dignity and goodness of man. The sense of his tragic
yearnings, his endless struggle to attain the perfection of a god, has
been bred, analyzed, or frozen out of them and been replaced by a
dazed contempt for his corruption and folly.[19]

These conclusions however fail to take into consideration the
major ideological position of the novelists – a position explicitly

---

[17]   Anton Myrer, *The Big War*, p. 104.
[18]   John T. Fredericks, "Fiction of the Second World War", *College English*, XVII (January, 1956), p. 197.
[19]   John W. Aldridge, *After the Lost Generation*, p. 132.

stated in Irwin Shaw's *The Young Lions*, a novel which both Fredericks and Aldridge deal with in their criticism. Michael Whitaker, clearly Shaw's spokesman in the novel, is rejected for OCS because of his slightly leftist leanings as a civilian. Asked if this does not disenchant or disillusion him with the war, Michael says that it does not, and explains: " 'When I went into the Army, I made up my mind that I was putting myself at the Army's disposal. *I believe in the war.* That doesn't mean I believe in the Army. I don't believe in any Army. You don't expect justice out of an Army, if you're a sensible, grown-up human being, you only expect victory.' " [20]

" 'I believe in the war.' " All of the ideological novelists either express or imply this belief; and the belief, on the one hand, negates Aldridge's and Fredericks' overly simply analyses of the novels, and on the other, distinguishes fundamentally the novels of the second World War from those of the first. The novelists are contemptuous of corruption and folly, as contemptuous as Dos Passos had been, or Cobb and Trumbo; but they saw their war not as a cause of these evils, rather as a crusade against them. They believed that they fought on the side of the right and the good, that Fascism, particularly the Nazi variety, had to be destroyed. They believed that while pain and death were saddening and bitter, they were not – or to state it more accurately, they need not be and had better not be – wasteful and unnecessary.

The novelists, like all social critics – like the social critics of the 1930's from whom they may legitimately be said to have evolved – are fundamentally hopeful and optimistic. Their optimism is expressed somberly and most often in the form of protest or warning, but it is no less hopeful for this: in the very ferocity of their criticism of corruption and folly they deny the futility of the struggle against them. The same statement can justly be made about the 1930's social protesters, about Steinbeck and Farrell and even Richard Wright. The same equally may be said of Cobb and Trumbo. They portrayed evil in order to fight it; they fought it in order to destroy it.

[20] Irwin Shaw, *The Young Lions*, p. 387.

Contrary to Aldridge's conclusion, the fight in both cases was motivated by a "basic belief in the dignity and goodness of man", and the evils fought against were those ideas, people, and institutions which denied or negated that belief. The depression writers labeled the evil, Conditions or the System; their villains were large or small men who might be willing to take advantage of the System for selfish reasons and at the expense of their fellow man. As a result, their social criticism struck out in all directions at once. There was no one thing, no one villain which received a concentrated attack. In James T. Farrell's *Studs Lonigan,* the villain is environment, and in his *My Days of Anger,* it is the oil interests; in Wessel Smitter's *F.O.B. Detroit,* it is production line working conditions; in Steinbeck's *In Dubious Battle,* it is the Have-Nots who are in the pay of the Haves; in Richard Wright's *Native Son,* it is racial prejudice and political intolerance. And in the World War I novels of the 1930's, as we have seen, war itself was the ultimate evil produced by the System.

By the mid-thirties, the System had achieved ideological status. To its selfish corruptness had been added brutality and aggressiveness; to its disregard of human rights and dignity had been added disdain for human life. All actions of the System were rationalized in terms of political or economic expediency, and all responsibility for the actions was removed from the individual and vested in the System. This was Fascism as the social critics of the thirties and as the World War II novelists defined or described it. It was the perfect ideological enemy, the embodiment and personification of all their enemies, since it represented an antithetical method of solving the same problems which the liberals were struggling to solve. Hitler came officially to power in 1933, the same year that Franklin Roosevelt took office, and the ideological battlelines were drawn. In 1935, Mussolini waged his Ethiopian campaign and the American Communist Party established the people's Front against Fascism, enlisting such notoriously uncommunistic social critics as Ernest Hemingway to the cause. From this date, the efforts of the majority of American liberals, both organized and unorganized, were bent toward the destruction of Fascism. But not until 1936 was the open challenge to physical struggle issued by Fascism. Spain was chosen as the battleground, and without hesitation, the liberals took up the gauntlet and declared, by word and deed, for the Loyalists.

The strength of the anti-Fascist impulse among American liberals was not tested until the signing of the Russo-German pact in 1939. The People's Front movement collapsed in the ensuing intra-ideological conflict. Granville Hicks led the liberal defection most articulately; Alfred Hayes, a John Reed Club poet, soon-to-be author of the war novels, *All Thy Conquests* and *The Girl on the Via Flaminea,* was at that time an editor of the *Patisan Review,* and was one of those who helped Hicks to pull that journal away from the far left on grounds that the pact was immoral. The People's Front split open, but the liberals closed ranks, united in their opposition to Fascism and disenchanted by Stalinism. War remained the ultimate social evil, but Fascism had to be destroyed, and physical violence had become the only means of destroying it. Thus, for the social critical novelists, war became at the very least a necessary evil.[21]

Irwin Shaw supplies a neat example of this shift in attitude. In 1936 (ironically, the year in which the Spanish Civil War began), he produced "Bury the Dead", a pacifist one-act play in which six dead soldiers in "the war that is to begin tomorrow" refuse to be buried because, as one of them puts it, " 'Maybe there's too many of us under the ground now. Maybe the earth can't stand no more. You go to change crops some time.' "[22] Generals, businessmen, and religions are blamed for the war and the deaths. The soldiers are cajoled and threatened; their women plead with them, a priest exorcises the devil possessing them, a General fires on them with a machinegun. But at the end, they simply walk off the stage, dead but unburied, to roam the world

[21]   Again, see Rideout and Aaron. It is interesting to note that Aldridge excludes the writers of the thirties from his discusion because he feels that "they had less effect and influence upon, and are more distantly related to, the writing of today" – which writing includes the war novels written through 1950.
[22]   Shaw, "Bury the Dead", in *Best Plays of 1936*, p. 66.

as an accusation of its stupidity. Significantly, they are followed off-stage by a number of live soldiers.

Yet in 1948, just twelve years after "Bury the Dead", Shaw marches the soldiers back onstage, angry and belligerent, to fight in that war that began tomorrow. *The Young Lions,* clearly because the System had become epitomized as Nazi-fascism, is a novel as emphatically pro-war as "Bury the Dead" and *Paths of Glory* and *Johnny Got His Gun* are adamantly anti-war.[20]

It should be noted however that the war novelists do not confine their social criticism to the battlefield enemy. Corruption, brutality, aggressiveness, irresponsible action for expedient reasons – these evils, in the aggregate and pushed to their extremes, constitute the terms for the novelists' definition of Nazi-Fascism, and the reasons for their crusade against it. But the evils are not the exclusive property of any nation or political philosophy, they could be found in Americans as well; many of the novelists, as we shall see, very clearly pin the Fascist label upon a few individual Americans and upon many of her institutions. And the best of the novelists were able to abstract the evil away from politics, to treat Fascism as a moral and ethical problem, and to see the war not only as a political conflict but as symbolic of a deeper ideological struggle between the forces of good and evil themselves.[24] Actual German and Italian Fascists, incipient American Fascists, were enemies that had to be destroyed; Fascism as a political philosophy had to be discredited.

But from the novelists' point of view, these were only the negative part of the means to a much more important end: the elimination of evil itself. The positive part of the means was the assertion of values to replace those destroyed and discredited,

[23] In 1946, Shaw produced *The Assassin,* a three-act play attacking Nazism and the sell-out of France by Vichy.

[24] Clearly, this is not a scientific definition, nor is it intended to be. The novelists were not concerned with Fascism as a political or economic entity or idea, but as a moral and ethical evil. And they felt that it must be identified and fought as such. Consequently, nowhere do they argue that it must be defeated and replaced by another political or economic philosophy or institution (by Democracy, for instance, or by Communism); rather they argue that it can be defeated only by individuals capable of recognizing the evil inherent in it.

and here the novelists break clearly away from politics and move into the realm of morals. They do not argue for replacing Fascism with any other political system or philosophy; they do argue for replacing it with individual responsibility. Their ideology resides in, emanates from, the individual, responsible, involved, committed. Like the war novelists of the 1920's, these men too settle upon the single irreducible segment of society as the only predictable unit of it; but the World War II novelists attempt to build society upon the individual rather than letting him reject his world and run from it. They seem to believe that they had a hand in making their world, and, taking their cue from the social critics of the 1930's, they argued that it was each man's duty to remake that world if and when it went wrong. The war was everyman's problem, and everyman had to fight it and win it and thereby make the world right again.

But largely because of their insistence upon individual responsibility in what they conceived to be a moral-ideological struggle, the World War II novelists generally avoid the traps which caught Cobb and Trumbo and many others of the social critical novelists of the thirties. They seldom lapse into sermonizing, though occasionally they allow their dialogue to follow lines perhaps too formally argumentative; their plots, with a few exceptions – notably, as we shall see, in *The Young Lions* – are not often theme-ridden. And, most importantly, their characterizations are almost never plot-ridden, even in the case of outright villains or of minor characters. The novelist's believe that the hope of the world resides in responsible individuals, or in individuals forced to accept responsibility, leads them away from the temptation, strong in the social critic, to create representational characters; leads them into the attempt to round their people off, to make them real and whole. Only such people can suffer doubt, can choose, and can commit themselves to their choice; only such people can sacrifice; only such people can be punished. Only such people, that is to say, can make the ideological novelists' message ultimately clear.

II. *THE CRUSADERS:* AN ARCHETYPE

By almost any measurement, one of the strongest novels to come out of the second World War was Stefan Heym's *The Crusaders*; as an ideological novel, it is especially strong. The book presents a sound overview of the European war, largely from the point of view of Third Army participation; at the same time it presents a significant insight into the motives and actions of a substantial cross-section of German and American soldiers and civilians. It is an ambitious novel, moving from Normandy through Luxembourg and into Germany, with an extended sidetrip to Paris during the days of liberation. It is therefore, necessarily extremely detailed, but for the most part, the details function integrally, as the means of clarifying the situation in which an individual character finds himself in order that an unmistakable if not inevitable ideological conclusion may be drawn from the details and the reaction of the character to them. In other words, Heym has not hung ideology on his novel but has let it grow out of the interaction of plot and character. Hence the strength of *The Crusaders* both as novel and as argument.

The character to whom the details of the novel come to mean the most, who filters them and chews them and through their effects comes to embody Heym's message, is Lt. David Yates. At the outset of the novel he is a compromiser, a man not lacking principles, but lacking integrity and the courage which can make principle operative. He is a complacent, lazy, lover of mental comfort who has convinced himself that the war and the struggle against Fascism are none of his business except in the most personal of senses. The German soldier, he says, has " 'got the

same trouble' " as the American: " 'Protecting his own posterior.' "
He does not know what the war is about; he does not care to
learn since he knows he won't believe what he learns anyway.
As a civilian, Yates had taught German at a small midwestern
university, and had embarked upon a reasonably successful career
by judicious politicking, and by making of himself a solid medi-
ocrity who could be relied upon to mind his own business and
take things slowly. His wife had wanted him to come out as
strong publicly as he did privately in support of the Loyalists is
the Spanish Civil War, but he refused on the grounds that it
might jeopardize his position. Through the course of the novel –
which begins in Normandy and ends in Germany, shortly after
the war has ended – primarily because of his association with
good men and evil, Yates' principles are so strengthened and his
conscience so enflamed that he is formed away from complacency
into action.

The cast of characters in the novel is enormous, but so integrally are they connected with the action and with Yates' conversion to responsibility that at least a few words must be said
about each of them. In his villains, Heym has personified every
aspect, both physical and philosophical, of the evil he opposes.
Oberstürmbannfuhrer Pettinger is a committed, diehard Nazi;
Lt. Col. Willoughby, junior law partner in an American firm
representing international steel interests, and Prince Yasha Bereskin, major stockholder in French and German steel, represent
the absolute amorality of international business; Mess Sgt. Dondolo is a sadistic, anti-semitic American enlisted man; Gen.
Farrish, division commander, is a stupid, vainglorious headline
grabber. All five of them are greedy; all five, but especially
Farrish, are ambitious. And all five justify their thoughts, words,
and actions in terms of expediency, tending at the same time to
reject whatever responsibility is rightly theirs to accept.

SS Col. Pettinger is utterly vicious but completely rational.
He knows what caused the rise of Nazism and coincidentally his
own rise:

The men who yammered and were depressed by a few defeats went
to pieces not so much because of nervous strain, but because their

horizon had the approximate reach of a toilet seat. When Pettinger compared the present state, even considering all that had happened in the past year and a half [i.e., 1943-44], with his pre-Nazi days – next morning's breakfast an uncertainly, no job, no future in sight, tramping the streets of his own country, turned away from the doors of factories and offices by men who claimed to be his countrymen – he knew that then he had known fear; and he shuddered even now, when he thought back to it. That had been the real fear; the fear of starvation, of becoming chaff, of losing one's hold over oneself, of dirt and disease and decay in a gutter.[1]

He knows where he is going, and he is certain of the result:

A thorough change could be brought about only by uprooting that permanent strata of life – only then would the peasant, the grocer, the clerk follow blindly, because there would be no place for him to return. The mass migrations from west to east, from east to west, the destruction of home and town, the creation of a new type of man – the barracks man, who had no home and who existed only to be worked and mulcted – were the real guarantees of a new time. They were the guarantees of ultimate National-Socialist victory, regardless of the issue of battle. And the Allies, the fools, were helping this new world on its way, by their invasion that turned Europe into a battlefield, by their mass bombings that daily destroyed more roots and daily decreased the strata of permanences. Let them come, with their fagged-out, outmoded institutions, let them try to set up once more a world as they knew it! It was impossible.

Yes, the storm he had helped to whip up might be only a lot of wind; but even wind, if it moved fast enough, could tear out and carry away the strongest trees.[2]

And later, after the defeat of Germany is complete, Pettinger is even more optimistic. " 'Play along with them!' " he advises the Allied-appointed mayor of Kremmen:

'Preserve for us what can be maintained. Because, beaten and defeated, we still hold the balance of power. But we must know where we're going! We must have a perspective! We must have a leadership, an organization that works through all channels – through what government the occupants permit us, though business, schools, the Church, through demobilized officers and returned prisoners of war. Slowly, playing one occupant against the other, making it difficult for them,

---

[1]   *The Crusaders*, p. 135.
[2]   *Ibid.*, p. 132.

rebuilding only what we need, patiently – until *Der Tag* when we'll spring forward, fullgrown, and dictate our terms!' [3]

For Heym, Col. Pettinger is the complete Nazi. He is cold, calculating, bitter, and ruthless – and not in the melodramatic or comic opera sense. There are plan and purpose in his reasoning, in his decisions, and in his actions. A Europe destroyed, a population without roots, an expediently hypocritical leadership – these are both the means and the ends of the Nazi ideology as Pettinger formulates it.

As allied troops move into Germany, he conceives of and sells the Generall Staff on a scorched earth policy under the slogan "*Not a Soul to the Enemy!*" As the enforcer of the policy, he uses not only propaganda techniques, but physical coercion as well. Those Germans who are not willing to desert and destroy their villages and homes are forced to do so at gunpoint. The people of a village named Ensdorf, for instance, refuse to leave, and hole up in an abandoned mineshaft. Pettinger cold-bloodedly orders the mine sealed by a dynamite blast.

His viciousness is bound in by no rules; a platoon of American soldiers captured by German tanks during the Battle of the Bulge is murdered at Pettinger's command. It is impractical to take prisoners.

Indicative of his danger as well as of his viciousness is Pettinger's murder of his commanding officer, Field Marshall Klemm-Borowski. The Marshall, having decided after the Ardennes failure that *Gotterdammerung* is at hand, places in Pettinger's hands a testament, beginning with the words "I die at the head of my troops to save Germany." He tells Pettinger that the testament argues that Germany's mistake had been in waging a two-front war, that the true enemy of all the Western world is Russia, and that the next war must find the West solidly together in a struggle with the East. In Pettinger, the Marshall believes, lies the hope of the new Germany. Pettinger realizes the full political value of the document, and realizes too that its value is greatly lessened unless Klemm-Borowski acutally dies. The chance that he will do so at the head of his troops is good, but

[3] *Ibid.*, pp. 528-29.

not perfect. Pettinger shoots him, calls it suicide, and charges the members of the Marshall's staff to give out the news that he died bravely in battle "so that Germany may live".[4]

Wittingly or unwittingly, the other villains plus some key minor characters, are important contributing factors to Pettinger's evil potential. Prince Yasha is the owner and operator of Delacroix and Cie., a mining and steel industry in France which is intimately associated with the German Rintelen Works. Yasha has cooperated fully with Vichy and with the Germans. " 'I have no loyalty to one or the other side' ", he says to Pettinger on the eve of the German retreat from Paris. " 'In order to become a traitor, one must have some loyalties, isn't that so?' " He and Pettinger come to an understanding: he helps Pettinger escape in return for Pettinger's promise to protect Delacroix's German interests from Nazi confiscation. Pettinger can give his promise because of his connections within the Nazi party, and because he is the commanding officer and friend of Major Dehn, the son-in-law of the widow Rintelen and, consequently, the head of German steel.

Major Dehn is captured upon the collapse of German hopes in the Bulge battle and he commits suicide rather than stand trial as a war criminal – they were his men whom Pettinger had ordered to massacre the American platoon. Pettinger assumes Dehn's identity with the connivance of the widow Rintelen – a stupid, frightened old woman whose vision extends no farther than the boundaries of the estate which her late industrialist husband had built from the profits of his munitions manufactures during both World Wars – and with the connivance of her nymphomaniac daughter, and of Herr Lammlein, the Allied-appointed Mayor of Kremmen, the city in which the Rintelen Works is located. Thus, Pettinger has assumed a position of great power immediately after the fall of Nazi Germany. But his position could not have been secured without the assistance of Willoughby and Farrish.

The General's evil results from a tendency to oversimplify coupled with ambition. After Farrish has discovered that a

[4]   *Ibid.*, pp. 481-88.

Parisian black market in gasoline has drained off his supplies
and kept his armor from moving past Metz, he calls angrily for
" 'a purge. We must weed out the undesirables – the crooks, the
politicians, the guys who talk back and always have dozens of
considerations. There is too much democracy in the Army, and
that doesn't work.' " [5]

He speaks these sentiments to Col. DeWitt, another American
who, like Lt. Yates, becomes convinced over the course of the
novel – largely through his exchanges with Farrish – that fascism
is a near and present danger; and who, in company with Yates,
finally acts to stop it.

" 'What do you mean by democracy?' " DeWitt asks, and
Farrish answers: " 'What I said. Talk, inefficiency, politics,
double-crossing, stealing my gas. A war has got to be run on
the basis of dictatorship – ' " And to DeWitt's disapproving stare,
he replies:

'You can't get around it old man! Afterwards, when there's peace,
they can have it all back – the politicians their politics, and the crooks
their graft. We've got to take our lesson from the enemy – much as
we might hate doing it. God, if one tenth of the gas sold in Paris had
been stolen on *their* side, hundreds of them would be lined up against
the wall, and justly so! My record is spotless, and yours is spotless,
and there are many others like us. Let's get together and clean out
that stable!' [6]

DeWitt hints that this is fascistic, and Farrish answers: " 'I don't
care what you call it. As long as it works' ", and DeWitt argues
that it does not work with the Germans, that " 'Fascism is the
most corrupt system ever.' " " 'I didn't say I wanted fascism' ",
Farrish replies. " 'If we want to win this war, it's got to be a
soldier's war, it's got to be handled of, by, and for soldiers.
Citizens' army . . . Sure, we've got to have citizens in it – whom
else? But soldiers have got to run it, according to the laws of a
soldier. . . .' " [7]

Such naivete becomes truly dangerous once the war has ended
and Farrish is commanding occupation troops in Kremmen, the

[5] *Ibid.*, p. 258.
[6] *Ibid.*
[7] *Ibid.*, p. 259.

city in which the Rintelen Works are located. The General has
" 'the best Division in the United States Army, and I'm going
to have the best occupation area in Germany' ". Results are what
he wants. He says to DeWitt:

'About city planning. I'm very much interested in that. Don't you see
the great chance we have. We can really do things here! If we had one
tenth that power in the States! Look at the mess there strikes! Here,
I put my finger on the map, and tommorow they start cleaning up
where I had my finger. You see results! For my money, the Krauts
aren't so bad. They're willing, they're accustomed to discipline.'

'You seem to know a lot about them.'

'What is there to know? I know Americans, don't I? Where's the difference?' [8]

Willoughby, the General's chief sycophant, has put the city, and
now wants to put the Rintelen Works, back into smooth operation – back, as Heym comments, into "a setup in which everybody has his place – the Chamber of Commerce men running
their businesses, and the other people working for them".[9] And
it matters not at all either to Willoughby or to Farrish, that these
were the same men who ran things under the Nazis. " 'Shall we
judge a man by a label, or by what he has done?' " asks the
newly-appointed Mayor Lammlein when Farrish, on orders from
Supreme Headquarters demands de-Nazification of the city ad-
ministration:

'Let him be punished, yes, for his weakness in having been a Nazi –
but let him be put to work rebuilding what his weakness help to
destroy! We cannot get the streetcars running without skilled personnel! We cannot begin to think of taking up production in the
Rintelen Works without the managerial talent required! Ultimately,
the decision is up to you, sir, you who have the greatness of mind to
weigh the importance of every one of us, you who have the interest
of the city at heart. I am sure, you will make the right choice.' [10]

And Farrish makes the expedient choice: " 'In our country we
have two Parties, and I haven't asked a single one of my officers

8   *Ibid.*, p. 573.
9   *Ibid.*, p. 551.
10 *Ibid.*, p. 553.

and men whether he's a Democrat or a Republican. To me, a man is a man, first; whatever else he is, comes after.'"[11] Ambition feeds his choice. Willoughby has convinced the General that he should allow himself to be drafted to run for Senator on the strength of the record he will make in Kremmen "'I thought you hated politicians'", DeWitt says, and Farrish answers: "'I'd be the politician to end all politicians. I've got my strategy all lined up. It's like at Avranches. I break through, and then there's no holding me.'" And "DeWitt's hand trembled slightly and he rested it on his knee. He was afraid of something. Not of Farrish, not of any one person – he didn't know of what."[12]

He obviously fears ambition, but ambition is not terribly dangerous unless it is coupled with unscrupulous cunning. The cunning which Farrish lacks, Willoughby is capable of supplying. He has taken control of Farrish for two reasons: First, because he truly sees the General as a potential political force, and secondly, because his proximity to the General is a good cover for his "'plunge into international cartelization'" with Prince Yasha and the Delacroix and Rintelen steel empires.

The Pettinger-Yasha alliance at the fall of Paris is repeated at its liberation by Yasha and Willoughby. A lawyer in civilian life, Willoughby has assumed the task of tying American and European steel interests together to the advantage of the law firm in which he is a junior partner. He calls on Yasha, knowing "that by no stretch of the imagination could his mission be called *in the line of duty*",[13] and explains "'that in the delicate balance

[11] *Ibid.*, p. 554.
[12] *Ibid.*, p. 574.
[13] *Ibid.*, p. 184. It is interesting to note that, in 1937, General Cummings of *The Naked and the Dead* performed a similar service for international chemical interests. War had not at the time been declared, but Mailer shows the effects of Cummings' machinations to be even more farreaching than Willoughby's: American foreign policy toward Spain is entrenched against the Loyalists through an industrial alliance with France – an alliance achieved through an appeal to the forces of conservatism and compromise which, inevitably, evolved into Vichy, the epitome of conservative compromise.
   Upon completing the agreement, Cummings says to Sallevoissiux, his French counterpart in the deal: "'What we're doing is really in the long-run what is best for France and America.'" "'Of Course, Major Cum-

of the play of free economic forces, lack of harmony, undue competition, and so on can be damaging not only to your House and to my friends whom I represent, but to the general task of reconstruction which confronts all of us' ".[14]

When Yasha asks for protection, says he fears Nationalization or Socialization of the steel industry, Willoughby sympathizes: " 'Nationalization, socialization – I don't give a damn what you call it – in effect, it means a decrease of efficiency which we cannot tolerate in an emergency situation. The Army needs the know-how of Management.' " [15] And later, when Yates, having discovered the alliance between Yasha and Willoughby, protests that it is undemocratic to permit an ex-collaborator to continue to operate so important an industry as steel, Willoughby answers that it is just the magnitude of the industry which makes it imperative to keep men like Yasha in control: " 'Democracy, Yates, is purely a matter of form. What we're concerned about, is: Will Yasha Bereskin, who knows about production and management, control the Delacroix mills? Or will it be a committee of the great unwashed, men from the DP camp, perhaps, who know only one thing – to work with their hands?' " [16]

In a nice bit or irony, Heym allows Yasha to suggest the danger that Willoughby – here, clearly, the American *alter ego* of the Nazi, Pettinger – represents:

Yasha could not help being amazed at Willoughby. What ability to blend a concern for the welfare of mankind with sound business practice! The Germans were orphans compared to it; they had covered their unashamed bullying and grabbing with love for the Fatherland – lately, they had dropped even that pretense. But the Americans really believed their own liberalism, at least this Major did. A healthy people. They had achieved the perfect amalgam of God, democracy, and the interest rate.[17]

It is a danger which Yates at this point in the novel is not strong

mungs' ", the Frenchman replies, " 'A peculiarly American statement, do you know?' " See *The Naked and the Dead*, pp. 421-24.

[14] *Ibid.*, p. 187.
[15] *Ibid.*, pp. 188-89.
[16] *Ibid.*, p. 292.
[17] *Ibid.*, p. 187.

enough to combat. And as Willoughby moves upward, promoted to Lt. Colonel after he has been named Farrish's Adjutant, it appears that he will remain impregnable. He protects Pettinger, who is posing as the Widow Rintelen's son-in-law, Pettinger controls the Rintelen Works. He works indefatigably toward a tripartite agreement among American, French, and German steel interests. "The war, after all, had been a good investment", he thinks. "Some people went in for paintings and diamonds, others collected cameras, or sold watches to the Russians, or soap and chocolate and cigarettes to the Germans. Small fry, breaking the law for petty booty. Laws were not made to be broken, laws were made to stay within. He had always maintained that war was like peace; except that in war the stakes were bigger, the opportunities greater. . . ." [18]

Mess Sgt. Dondolo is one of the small fry, along with Capt. Loomis, second in command to Willoughby and Lt. Yates' immediate commanding officer. These two are mixed up in the Parisian black market, dealing in, among other things, Farrish's gasoline. Their contact is a Frenchman named Sourire, who also happens to be a hireling of Prince Yasha and the man whose truck was used to effect Pettinger's escape from Paris. Both Dondolo and Loomis are brutes. Loomis rapes a French girl during the victory celebration in Paris. Dondolo attempts to rape a German girl who has come to offer the surrender of the people of Ensdorf whom Pettinger has ordered sealed in the mine. The girl escapes Dondolo, and, because of her experience, the people of Ensdorf try to retreat up into Germany, only to be caught in a murderous artillery barrage. As an almost direct result of Dondolo's brutality, they are all killed.

In addition, Dondolo is almost violently anti-semitic; his opening gambit to all Jews is "Vot ees it?" and he says to Sgt. Bing, a naturalized American of German-Jewish parentage:

'It's because of people like you I had to leave my kids. If anything happens to them, I'll kill you. Bunch of Jews get themselves into trouble, and the whole American Army swims across the ocean. This fellow Hitler, he knew what he was doing, and Mussolini, he, too.

[18] *Ibid.*, p. 598.

Everything is wrong. We should be fighting with them, against the Communists!' [19]

Finally, and predictably, Dondolo is a sadist. Thorpe, a wounded veteran of the African campaign whose wounding destroyed his courage is the victim of the Mess Sgt's. viciousness. He takes terrible physical and mental punishment, and when Dondolo is apparently trapped as a black marketeer, he gets off the book by framing Thorpe. Jailed, Thorpe collapses mentally, and ends in a mental institution, perhaps permanently in shock.

Clearly, Heym draws a parallel between his ugly Americans and fascism. The brutality of Dondolo, the ambition of Farrish, the expedient amorality of Willoughby are combined in the Nazi, Pettinger; but they are no less evident for being disseminated among Americans, and no less dangerous. Thorpe, victim, sooth-sayer, mad Jeremiah makes this point at the novel's very be-ginning. " 'Dondolo!' " he cries after his first run-in with the Mess Sgt.:

'He's just one of them! It goes up all the way!. . . . Willoughby, Farrish! I've seen Farrish come through our hospital in North Africa. There was a guy with shock, crazy. The guy stands before his bed, at attention, and has to listen to Farrish calling him names. After-wards, they had to take the guy to the other ward where they don't allow visitors. I tell you, I was grateful I at least had a couple of honest-to-goodness shrapnel holes in my body to show.' [20]

And a few pages further on, Thorpe crashes an officers' party to tell his fears and issue his warning to Lt. Yates:

'You're an honest man. . . . You're in the same boat. Don't you see this war is being lost? We're losing it every day. The fascists are all over us. I'm not sick. I see it, with my own eyes I see it, creeping up on us. Right here, in this room, in this Chateau, in this Army, at home. . . . ' [21]

Immediately after this outbreak, Yates "rescues" Thorpe from the ire of the other officers by turning him over to the custody

---

[19]   *Ibid.*, p. 37.
[20]   *Ibid.*, p. 40.
[21]   *Ibid.*, p. 57.

of Dondolo, who, as soon as he has Thorpe alone, beats him unmercifully.

Significantly, it is Yates to whom Thorpe addresses his warning, and it is Yates who, out of misguided charity, turns Thorpe over to evil. Because he has decided to remain passive, rejecting responsibility, refusing to see the evil around him – though refusing as well to be a part of it – Yates is only dimly aware of the consequences of his inaction. Heym relentlessly pounds awareness into him over the course of the novel, putting him into relatively close contact with evil, from Farrish, his commanding General, through Willoughby, the commanding officer of the Prapaganda Intelligence Detachment, to Dondolo, the Detachment's Mess Sgt., letting him become conscious gradually of the motives as well as the actions of each man. Heym never lets Yates rest in his complacency. He gives him the memory of the three-monkey statue his wife had placed on his desk; he gives him warts on the hands which bother Yates terribly when he is nervous; he gives him the soothsayer-victim, Thorpe, a walking conscience.

And he gives Yates other good people, many of them victims as well. The intricate meshing and interweaving of evil which becomes part of Yates' experience is juxtaposed to a developing consciousness of good fed by a number of admirable people who surround him even more intimately than do the evil people. There is Tolachian, too old to fight, but who fights anyway because "'When you see a bad weed, you tear it out, roots and all. Otherwise it will swallow the whole field'",[22] and who is killed because Yates did not insist strongly enough that a younger man should have been given his assignment.

There is Mme. Glodin, the French schoolteacher at Isigny whose house has been destroyed and whose son has been left a cripple, but who can declare that "'It was worth while to lose everything just to see the Boches run.'"[23] About her, Yates says: "'When the war's over . . . and it is going to be over someday . . . how will they ever live together? So much hate! A school-

22   *Ibid.*, p. 41.
23   *Ibid.*, p. 22.

teacher talking that fanatically!' " [24] But recalling her a short time later, he thinks: "there must be something more to it than he, himself, knew or cared to admit." [25]

There is Kavalov, an escaped Russian slave laborer in a German coal mine who had led a May Day strike and had been hung by the wrists and flogged; who had escaped to become a guerilla fighter, eventually joining American troops in Germany for a short time, then drifting off to fight in his own way again. He becomes a symbol for Yates of dogged purposefulness, of joyful certainty of the rightness of the present and the glory of the future – a symbol of all of the things which Yates has not felt or known and, at the end, wants desperately to feel and know. On the Russian side of the Elbe, getting drunk with Russian troops, Yater toasts the missing Kavalov;

> ' . . . you have the joy. Maybe the joy doesn't come from resting and looking back. Maybe it comes with looking ahead, seeing life as a struggle, burning yourself out in it, giving yourself to it. You're a sonofabitch. You forced me into this. I didn't want it. I was content. I thought I'd done enough. But all right. We'll go on from here, you, and I. Only give me your joy. Give it to me: I need it. . . . ' [26]

There is DeWitt, whose soul-searching parallels Yates', and who arrives with Yates at the decision to act. There is Capt. Troy, honest, tough, part of whose company was massacred at Pettinger's order. Simply by being what he cannot help being, by suffering but continuing to fight, Troy teaches Yates that "You can't be just a sharer of burdens. . . . You must work with people, join in with people, be one of them, even if you have to trim some of your finery." [27]

There is Thérèse Laurent, violated by Loomis, who teaches Yates that the major part of loving is the giving of oneself, is caring enough to submerge the self at least partly in the loved one. Her traumatic experience with Loomis has frozen Thérèse; Yates thaws her by caring more for her than for himself, and in

[24]   *Ibid.*, p. 23.
[25]   *Ibid.*, p. 31.
[26]   *Ibid.*, p. 512.
[27]   *Ibid.*, p. 492.

the process, he finds that, deny it or reject it though he may, he *does* feel responsible for things and people outside himself.

There is Kellermann, ex-concentration camp inmate, now displaced person living in Kremmen with hundreds of others in a hovel called the Lower Depths. He has no work, no home, no clothes; he is only slightly better off under the Americans than he was under the Nazis – especially since, as we have seen, the town is being run by ex-Nazis anyway. When Yates offers to help him, Kellermann refuses, explaining: " 'It isn't me at all. It's many people – thousands, tens of thousands – people who would help you to make this country into something decent. . . . No, Lieutenant, I don't think I'll accept your charity. I'll leave this place when everybody else is getting out of it.' " [28]

Yates' offer is a futile, empty gesture toward the elimination of gross injustice. It is made off the cuff; it results from, and can result in, no real plan of action, and once Kellermann has rejected it, Yates has no alternate suggestion. He can do nothing about the DPs in general because the Army has made no preparations for dealing with their problem. The Army has improvised each time it has been presented with an embarrassing or trying situation, and each time the results have been extremely unsatisfactory. When the people of Ensdorf ask for aid, the Army must hesitate because it is totally unprepared for such an eventuality, and the hesitation coupled with Dondolo's viciousness results in the massacre of the people; the Army occupies the city of Kremmen, then finds that there are no plans for setting up a proper civil government, so the ex-Nazis gravitate toward the positions of power; when the inmates of Paula Concentration Camp are liberated, they wind up in the Lower Depths, the grossest improvisation of all.

By the time of his interview with Kellermann, Yates has come to recognize his own prior indifference to the evil around him as responsibility for the evil, has come finally to commit himself unselfishly to the Crusade. As the interview closes, he knows that such commitment is not enough, that some real action must take place, and that it must be concerted action since the individual

[28] *Ibid.*, p. 545.

alone is powerless in the face of evil. He knows, finally, that
there must be a conspiracy of good corresponding to the conspiracy of evil which is closing in upon him.

This knowledge has been building in Yates for a long time;
Kellermann merely crystalizes it for him. Sgt. Bing, the most
important of the good-victims in the novel, and the major antagonist to Yates' conscience, has the knowledge from the beginning, and tries to convince Yates of it. Bing and Yates work
together as interrogators of German prisoners, but Yates thinks
of the prisoners as " 'poor slobs' ", victims of their " 'politicians
as we're the victims of ours' "; while Bing, dispossessed German-
Jew, simply and frankly hates them. " 'Hate . . . ' ", Yates says,
" 'This is a scientific war. You want to understand the Germans,
don't you? If you have to guage their state of mind, you have
to put yourself in their place. How can you, if you hate them?' "
" 'You talk like the German prisoners' ", Bing replies. " 'They
believe they know what they're fighting for, and they think we
don't!' " Yates' retort reflects his thinking at the outset of the
novel: " 'They don't either. Nobody knows. You start out into
the war equipped with newspaper headlines. Flimsy stuff.' " [29]

Here is the key to the conspiracy of good, Bing knows: Belief,
awareness of the reasons for the war and a solid commitment to
the fight. When General Farrish proposes to fire 48 rounds from
48 guns on the Fourth of July – the final round containing a
propaganda leaflet to be written by the Propaganda Intelligence
Detachment stating American war aims – Yates protests (not to
the General, however) that the plan is puerile and obviously
intended only to gain publicity for Farrish. He protests too, because "the leaflet imposed upon him the necessity of facing
questions he was not prepared to answer". " . . . what we are
fighting for was a maze of motives, some clear, some hidden,
some idealistic, some selfish, some political, some economic . . .
one would have to write a book instead of a leaflet; and . . . even
then, the issue would be anything but straight".[30]

But Bing disregards the General's motives, rejects Yates'

29   Ibid., pp. 9-10.
30   Ibid., p. 15.

cynicism, and seizes the opportunity to explain his beliefs to his former countrymen. He writes the leaflet, and it is fired. It reads, in part:

On July Fourth, 1776, the United States was born as a nation – a nation of free men, equal before the law, and determined to govern themselves.

For these rights and liberties, we went to war in 1776. For these rights and liberties, we are fighting today. For, wherever they are threatened, we are threatened. Wherever the dignity of Man is affronted, we feel that it happens to us. Wherever people are oppressed and suffering, we are affected. Because we are that kind of nation, we haven come to Europe to stop a tyrant from imposing his will on a nation, on Europe, and on the whole world.[31]

The naivete so evident here grates on Yates' sophistication, but jars his conscience as well; and Bing continues to keep that conscience off balance. It is Bing, for example, who convinces Yates of the criminality of improvisation, and who challenges him to do something about it – something more than throwing up his hands in horror or disgust. It is Bing, as much as Thérèse Laurent, who shows Yates the relationship between love and responsibility. After visiting Neustadt, the German city of his birth and youth, and finding its people hopelessly corrupted by Nazism, Bing loses his enthusiasm, his hope, and lapses into a cynical depression. It takes some time for Yates to realize the seriousness of Bing's condition, but when he does, he sees clearly his responsibility: "He knew Bing needed help, now, or at least straightening-out, and he had learned that in war this help is an obligation as holy as that of the medic who pulls you, wounded, out of the line. He had denied it to Thorpe, once; he had paid the penalty",[32] – the penalty of a tortured conscience.

Bing is killed, the victim of a carelessness which results from his depression, before Yates can help him. But his death is far from tragic really, since it functions as a sacrifice by means of which Yates is brought to feel committed to the Crusade. Bing,

[31] *Ibid.*, p. 63. In a "Note" to the novel, Heym points out that such a leaflet actually was fired on July 4, 1944.
[32] *Ibid.*, p. 491.

Kellermann, Thérèse Laurent, Thorpe – through these people primarily, through the challenge they present to his conscience, through their replies to his doubts, through the hope they present to counter his cynicism, Yates is spurred onward toward the destruction of Pettinger, the discrediting of Willoughby, and the sidetracking of Farrish's political express.

In the last pages of *The Crusaders*, all of the antagonists and protagonists, with the exception of Bing, Thérèse Laurent, and Dondolo are brought together for an extended climax and denouement. Heym relies on sound characterization and motivation, rejecting coincidence and surprise to bring about an ending which is a marvel of artistic efficiency – if these are not mutually exclusive terms – and, more importantly, to reinforce an ideological statement which he has made unmistakably clear long before the ending.

As the weakness of the human condition had held Yates aloof from involvement in the struggle with evil, that same weakness in Pettinger and Willoughby makes them vulnerable once Yates has engaged himself. Willoughby, drifting on a wave of false security, succumbs to greed, cutting himself in on the graft which Loomis collects from the merchants of Kremmen for allowing them to stay in business. This is a weakness which a less complacent Willoughby would call "petty", but which is inherent in the greed that is his single strongest motivation. Part of his complacency comes from his having taken Marianne Seckendorff, a supposed political victim of the Nazis, as his mistress. Willoughby places her in the Rintelen mansion, where she is at once respectable and handy. But Pettinger is there, posing as the dead Major Dehn and, predictably enough if one considers his coldly sadistic tendencies, Pettinger's overriding weakness is lust.

The explosion is ready, and Yates now is ready for it. Out of jealousy, Pamela Dehn exposes Marianne to Yates, and in the process, unwittingly exposes Pettinger too, for Yates knows that the real Major Dehn is dead. And when Willoughby refuses to protect her, Marianne tells Yates about the graft collections. The means of action having been presented to him, Yates moves rapidly into battle. He and Capt. Troy trap an armed Pettinger

in an air raid shelter, and, unwilling to risk anyone's life to capture him, seal the exits with dynamite – an action clearly reminiscent of Pettinger's order to do the same to the people of
Ensdorf. Yates presents his documented charges of graft to
DeWitt who presents them to Farrish for action:

'General, in your nice clean Dragoon Barracks, in your nice, comfor-
table apartment. you've been presiding over a nest of corruption that's
falling apart right now, under your very eyes that never saw a sign of
it. You don't see anything because you're smug as all hell, sitting on
top of your victories and forgetting that they're not an end in themselves, but a means to an end. Well, maybe you didn't forget it. But
the end that you have in mind: to use them to climb higher, to become
Senator or Governor of your State and maybe President of the whole
United States – that's not the end that counts.' [33]

Farrish, convinced, dismisses Willoughby and transfers him back
to the States. And with Willoughby goes Farrish's hope of immediate political achievement; the possibilities of scandal are
far too great.

Yates has won, but his victory is highly qualified. Pettinger
is dead, the Rintelen estate has been turned over to the people
of the Lower Depths. But Dondolo and Willoughby have simply
been shipped back to the States, the Mess Sgt. with his black
market gains in the bank, the Colonel with the Rintelen shares
and his cartelization – which, incidentally, is Yasha Bereskin's
protection – safely in his pocket. When a spokesman from the
Lower Depths, an ex-university Professor, thanks the Americans
for the Rintelen estate in these terms: " 'We learned [in Paula
contration camp] that the enemy does not necessarily come from
across any front lines or borders. What do we want, what have
we always wanted? A country in which men and women can live
free of fear, secure in their lives, their ideas, and the fruits of
their work.' " Farrish replies: " 'What the Professor here has said
is well and good, and I approve of it. I've always approved of
noble sentiments. But with all of that, a person's got to know
his place. . . . ' " [34]

[33]   *Ibid.*, pp. 628-29.
[34]   *Ibid.*, p. 641.

Farrish has really learned nothing; his furious ambition has simply been cooled down. And Willoughby – as he leaves for Le Havre and shipment home, thinks "They imagined they had won – Yates, DeWitt, the whole faction of Crusaders. But they hadn't. They couldn't win. They would never win."

The qualified victory serves to reinforce Heym's message by investing it with urgency. The physical struggle has ended with the death of Pettinger, but the ideological struggle, the struggle against the force of evil which Pettinger epitomized, must continue. And the struggle can be carried on successfully only by the Yates' and Bings, the Troys and DeWitts – by enlightened, committed individuals willing to involve themselves in a collective effort.

The Crusaders is perhaps the most 'complete' of the World War II novels. It portrays combat action vividly; it deals carefully with the psychological effects of war in the characterizations of Thorpe and Bing. It emphasizes accuracy of detail, even to introducing disguised but easily identifiable people as characters – General Farrish is quite obviously patterned after General George S. Patton, for example. And most importantly, it is a serious ideological novel, with many of the flaws as well as perfections of the novels in that category.

As the preceding discussion shows, the novel is intricate, lengthy, and quite involved, primarily because Heym desires to leave no questions unanswered, to set forth as clearly as possible his ideological position. Indeed, the discussion has hardly been exhaustive; a great many characters and incidents which function integrally in the story have not been dealt with here, largely because the discussion itself would become too intricate and unwieldy.

Such intricacy may be the novel's major flaw. It probably lies lies behind the fact that the novel never achieved real popularity. Other lengthy and involved books were written, *The Naked and the Dead,* for example, and *The Young Lions*; but Shaw's story is episodic rather than intricate, and Mailer's is tied together by technique, by special effects, as it were. *The Crusaders* on the other hand is a straight-forward nineteenth century type of narrative in which the intricacies are collated and meshed to form the whole. It is not the sort of novel one can put down for a time and then move into again; it demands a concentrated effort which not too many readers are willing any longer to exert.

Finally, *The Crusaders* is very nearly the archetype of the ideological war novels, for it embodies the characterizations, the arguments, and the conclusions present in all of them. Therefore, despite its relative obscurity – and with no intent to downgrade the other novels – I have made it the key book in this discussion. The ensuing chapters sort out the elements of ideology which inform *The Crusaders,* label them, and discuss the other war novels in terms of each element.

III. THE FIRST FACE OF VILLAINY

One of the most notable fatures of the ideological war novels, growing out of the novelists' strong desire to sit in moral judgment upon Fascism, is the presence in them of identifiable villainy and villains. Pettinger, Willoughby, Dondolo in *The Crusaders*; Christian Diestl, Lt. Hardenburg in *The Young Lions*; the Questore of Rome in *All Thy Conquests*; General Cummings, Sgt. Croft in *The Naked and the Dead* – each of these characters is an active personification of evil; each is therefore clearly a villain. But because some of them are Germans and Italians while others are Americans, they actually represent two aspects of that evil, two similar though distinct faces of villainy embodying two distinct sets of implications. Thus it seems wise, while examining each face at some length here, to treat each separately.

Actual German, Italian, or Japanese characters – the first face of villainy – are relatively rare in the war novels. They are difficult to draw realistically, without melodrama; it takes a breadth of political awareness, and a peculiarly paradoxical combination of objective distance and personal involvement to create a more than two dimensional Nazi or fascist villain, a Pettinger or a Christian Diestl. Most of the novelists, perhaps wisely, declined to try.

None of them, not even the most politically sophisticated such as Norman Mailer, tried to create a Japanese ideological villain. The reason is deceptively simple: the novelists, like the ordinary soldier, saw the Japanese as stupid, impetuous upstarts who had begun a war that they could not possibly win for reasons that were never very clear. They were never considered an ideological enemy largely because their ideology was a mystery. They were not Fascist, despite their alliance with the Germans and Italians, and no attempt was made in any of the war novels to super-impose this Western ideology on their motives. The extension of the Japanese Empire as an ideological threat, unlike the potential extension of Nazi-Fascism, never occurred to the novelists.

However, the Japanese were an extremely dangerous physical enemy who fought a totally defensive war hard and viciously, and they were portrayed as such in the novels. They retreated to the tops of trees or into holes in the ground from which they sniped and counterpunched. They raided at night, in silence, or they charged screaming forward in banzai attacks. They fought like trapped animals, and it was very much as animals that they were described in the novels. The American soldier seldom saw the Japanese as human beings but only as stupid, half-civilized things which he despised for causing the misery of jungle war-fare, and killed out of self-preservation, fear, and an impersonal but pervasive hatred. And the novelists generally reflected the soldiers' attitude with accuracy; as Peter Bowman put in in *Beach Red*: "Do unto Japs as Japs do unto you – but first."

Some of the novelists tried unsuccessfully to soften this feeling. Francis Irby Gwaltney lets the hero of *The Day the Century Ended*, Sam Gifford, rebel mentally against his Colonel's pom-pous statement that " 'There'll be good hunting, men' ", in his pep talk just prior to the invasion of Leyte. Gifford thinks: "as much as we hated the Japs, we couldn't help thinking of them as humans. The idea of their being game sickened me." [1] But as the novel proceeds the fighting becomes more fierce, and good men are wounded – physically, emotionally – or killed through the terror of jungle warfare, and Sam's feelings change consider-ably. He is hardly touched, let alone sickened, as a buddy searches through the mouths of dead Japanese for gold teeth – once even, Sam watches impassively as he pulls the teeth of an unconscious Jap soldier, then shoots him through the head.

Carl Jonas attempts to plumb Japanese reasoning in *Beach-*

[1] Francis Irby Gwaltney, *The Day the Century Ended*, p. 195.

head on the Wind, a novel concerned with the building of an airstrip on Tartu in the Aleutians. When unopposed Japanese aircraft refuse to attempt the destruction of the Seebee dock, Jonas guesses that they simply do not want to risk losing a plane:

Perhaps this is a national trait . . . to hang onto their proud constructions. They are so young in the world of modern enterprise, so proud
of their achievements, and hold the symbols of their progress in such
childlike veneration. Time after time they have done this. At Tarawa
they failed to destroy the jetty thrown out past the coral reef . . . the
one lane which proved practicable for the Marine advance ashore and
without which our men might never have landed, or at least would
have landed with three times the loss of life which was great enough
as it was, the Japs thus losing face, island, and five thousand troops,
the best they ever had. It disturbed us all, but then we are queer
people, too. Perhaps the Japs over Tartu were simply cold, sick, of
this corner of the world, and fouled up like everyone else in the
North.[2]

Such a tenuous resolution of his mystification leaves Jonas as far removed from an understanding of Japanese thinking and motivation as ever. A few pages further on in the novel, a sailor named O'Higgins discovers and kills a Japanese soldier who had apparently been landed on Tartu for reconnaisance purposes. The description of the killing betrays no searching feelings for the Japanse by Jonas through O'Higgins or any other of his characters. The soldier is stabbed with a boat hook, then his skull is cracked with its haft, and finally he is shot with his own gun. One of the men on the burial detail, like Sam Gifford's buddy, steals the gold fillings which had been knocked from the mouth of the dead man, and uses them to play an elaborate gold-mine hoax on the Chief Petty Officer in charge of the work crews on the island.

Norman Mailer introduces a Japanese prisoner as a human being – frightened, hungry, thirsty, grateful – into *The Naked and the Dead,* but Mailer does not make of him a character, for his purpose is to illustrate the sadism of Sgt. Croft, not to give the reader a greater understanding of the Japanese enemy. Croft, in mounting excitement, bids the prisoner to sit down, feeds him

---

[2] Carl Jonas, *Beachead on the Wind,* pp. 83-84.

a chocolate bar and water, looks at a picture of his wife and two children, gives him a cigarette and lights it for him – then shoots him in the head. The episode, for all its apparent sympathy for the enemy soldier, casts considerable light on Croft's character, but none at all on the Jap's:

Croft stared for almost a minute at the Jap. His pulse was slowing down and he felt the tension ease in his throat and mouth. He realized suddenly that a part of his mind, very deeply buried, had known he was going to kill the prisoner. . . . He felt quite blank now. The smile on the dead man's face amused him, and a trivial rill of laughter emitted from his lips. 'Goddam', he said. . . . and he prodded the body with his foot, 'Goddam', he said, 'that Jap sure died happy'. The laughter swelled more strongly inside him.[3]

These three novelists display as much understanding of the Japanese enemy as is to be found in any of the books to come out of the war in the Pacific. It is insufficient for the creation of either a truly sympathetic or a truly villainous character. Only when we come to the occupation novels such as MacKinlay Kantor's *Don't Touch Me* and James Michener's *Sayonara*, are we shown the Japanese as human beings. Yet even here, we find no suggestion that they had been an ideological enemy. Their motives in fighting the war are as mysterious and incomprehensible to the occupation writers as they were to the war novelists. As a matter of fact, it is with obviously pleasant surprise that the occupation novelists find the Japanese to be sensitive and highly civilized human beings, once they are out of the jungle and away from the war. They are portrayed understandingly, sympathetically, humanely; there is not even a hint of villainy in the portrayals.

But the European war was fought in civilized territory, much of it in the homelands of the enemy. German and Italian cities became battlegrounds; their civilians were part of the action, as participants or victims. There was no jungle neutral ground on which the physical struggle could take place. Moreover, the Germans and Italians posed a distinct ideological threat. Their beliefs were not strange and mysterious, barbaric though they

---

[3] Mailer, *The Naked and the Dead*, pp. 194-95.

might be. The Nazi-Fascist ideology ran counter to what the novelists considered to be the ideological direction of a progressive Western civilization. Dictatorship, concentration camps, mass murder, total war – these manifestations of the Nazi-Fascist ideology were perversions or corruptions of the heritage of the Western world. And they were corruptions conceived by Western peoples rather than by peoples of another race and culture. The Germans and Italians could be held accountable for the perversions, as any criminal who knows the law can be held responsible for wilfully breaking it. The Japanese could not, really; there was no certainty even that they subscribed to the law – there was indeed, on the basis of the experience of jungle warfare, a strong suspicion that they did not even know the law. To put the situation another way: the American soldier, and the novelists, could see the Japanese only as animals acting like animals; but the Nazi-Fascist enemies were human beings who had wilfully, and criminally, chosen to be animals. Their responsibility, their guilt, was ultimately greater.

For all of these reasons, it was possible for the American novelists to create German and Italian villains as personifications or epitomes of ideological evil, while it was impossible for them to create Japanese villains of the same nature.

However, it was nearly as difficult to create an Italian villain as a Japanese, though for entirely opposite reasons. For all practical purposes, Italy had retired from the war by the time America got into it – if indeed, upon the evidence of her fiascos in western France and Greece she had ever really been in it. She was never the physical enemy that either Japan or Germany were. The battles of Africa, Sicily, and Italy were waged primarily against German troops. Neither was Italy an ideological enemy comparable to the Germans, though certainly, she was more so than the Japanese. She was clearly a Fascist state, totally undemocratic. Political terrorism and reprisal were common occurrences while she flourished and even after she began her collapse, as witness the execution of Count Ciano. But slave labor, concentration camps, persecution of Jews were largely German, Nazi refinements added to the Fascist ideology.

Principally for these two reasons, the Italian people generally were treated by the novelists with a kindness and sympathy similar to that with which the occupation novelists treated the Japanese. John Horne Burns, in *The Gallery,* finds an attractive sort of *Weltschmerz* in the actions of the Italians – love is sadly beautiful, hate is sadly bitter, sin is committed knowingly but with infinite sadness. They are naive yet terribly sophisticated children whose naivete is far from innocence, but almost equally far from guilt; they never believe that sin will solve their problems, but they know that innocence will not solve them either. " 'Sometimes' ", Michael Patrick says:

'I like you Eyeties better than I do my own. There's something good and gentle in most of you. Where are we going in this war? I don't know, for all the orientation talks they used to give us. There's something about Italy and you Eyeties that gets me. There's dirt and poverty here. But there's something else that gets me. Seems to survive your battered towns and your bitter men and your degraded women. Why is all this? Why must it be? Something terrible has come into this world.' [4]

The Gallery is a frame novel, a collection of stories concerning people who visit the Galleria Umberto Primo in Naples shortly after the liberation of that city. Most of the visitors, like Michael Patrick are with the Allied armies. Their stories seldom intersect or interlock; their presence in the Gallery, at one time or another, is all that binds the stories together.

Giulia, a proper young girl, is the only truly major Italian character in *The Gallery.* She is the only daughter of an honest Italian family forced by the circumstances of war into poverty. Her father had worked for the State, but in a clerical, non-political capacity; her younger brother, for quite non-political reasons, spends his evenings "rolling" drunken GIs. Giulia goes to work as a cashier in an American officer's club where, be-

[4] Burns, *The Gallery,* p. 10. John Hersey, *A Bell for Adano,* and Elliott Arnold, *Tomorrow Will Sing,* caught the naïveté of the Italians but apparently did not sense or disregard the profound awareness of them which so impressed Burns and Hayes. For Hersey and Arnold, the Italians are simply highly sentimental children whose hurts and desires are easily satisfied by an obvious symbol like a bell, or by direct proof like a radio broadcast.

tween making change and fending off passes, she dreams of old-fashioned love and romance. She falls in love eventually with an ugly American captain who possesses a tender soul, and leads him into her kind of courtship, refusing even to stay with him on the last night before his return to battle. But she knows that he will come back to her. There is no suggestion of physical or ideological villainy here; Giulia's "cruelty" is universally female, and has nothing to do with politics. Burns enjoyed writing sentimentally; besides "Giulia", many of the stories in *The Gallery* so testify. But *The Gallery* is a better novel than this story would indicate, and we will return to discuss it more at length in connection with the second face of villainy.

Alfred Hayes, in both *The Girl on the Via Flaminea* and *All Thy Conquests,* reacts to ordinary Italians with the same sympathy and compassion as does Burns, though his treatment of situations similar to Giulia's somewhat more realistic. Lisa, in *The Girl on the Via Flaminea,* is one of the good and the gentle who is morally and psychologically maimed by the war. She sins hopelessly, in order to prevent the dirt and poverty, becoming the lover and pretended wife of an American soldier when she had never before met. Her friend, Nina, consort of American officers, arranges the liaison and convinces Lisa of its necessity and rightness: " 'One doesn't live as one likes to, but as one must. Go through the city. On the Corso, on the Via Veneto, on all the bridges – it's the same. Everywhere the soldiers and the women. Why? Because there is nothing else, cara mia, except to drink and to make love and to survive.' " [5]

But the argument is not convincing enough. Lisa submits, but finds no happiness in her role as hired mistress. Even though Robert, the soldier, grows more warmly and sincerely attached to her, she cannot help feeling that she is little more than a prostitute. And when the American Military Police discover the deception, arrest her, force her to take a physical examination and thenceforward to carry the yellow identification card of the prostitute, she can no longer justify the arrangement with Robert. She leaves, going apparently toward the bridges, either to leap

[5]   Hayes, *The Girl on the Via Flaminea*, p. 29.

or to pursue openly the profession which she feels she has been practising.

In *All Thy Conquests,* Hayes presents Carla, a sweet young girl somewhere between Lisa and Burns' Giulia: like Giulia, she loves her American soldier, and like Lisa – but for love – she sleeps with him. On the day that she intends to announce to the soldier that she is pregnant, he, in a fit of remorse, tells her that he is married and breaks off their relationship. She does not make her announcement, and on her way home, distracted, she falls out of one of the trucks used as busses in Rome during the war, and miscarries.

And in the same novel, Hayes portrays Giorgio, a middle-aged non-combattant Italian who is anxiously struggling to reattain his pre-war position and dignity in a Rome physically and economically in ruins. Giorgio has sunk to attacking and rolling drunken soldiers, stealing boots and clothing as well as money, partly as a means of making a living and partly as compensation for his lowered station.

Giorgio is hardly a warm character; hardly as sympathetic as Lisa or Carla. But he is by no means a villain either, certainly not an ideological villain. Het is a sensitive human being, hurt terribly by the war and reacting to the hurt; there is not the slightest suggestion that Fascism motivates his actions.

Nonetheless, *All Thy Conquests* is one of the most powerful ideological novels to come out of the war, primarily because its principal character *is* a Fascist villain. Like *The Gallery,* it is a frame novel, at the heart of which is the war-crimes trial of the Italian Questore of Rome. He is being tried because, upon the order of the German officer in command of the city, he had submitted a list of 350 innocent Italian civilians – ten for each member of a German patrol which had been wiped out by the underground – for retaliatory execution. The 350 men, women, and children had been machine-gunned in a sandpit at the outskirts of Rome. Upon this frame are hung the stories of Carla and Giorgio. Upon it too are hung the stories of Harry, an American infantryman who searches fruitlessly for the nameless Italian girl who had been sweet to him on the day of liberation, before the fighting took him further north to be wounded; of the Marchese Aldo Alzani, decadent aristocrat, homosexual, negative and destructive force who drives his Italian Army General father-in-law to suicide, and who drives his wife into an affair with a neo-Fascist politician – all for his personal gain; and of Captain Pollard, attached to the Allied government of Rome, whose world is shattered when his American Red Cross mistress decides to return to her husband. The stories are unrelated; except incidentally, there is very little interaction among the characters – Pollard, having drowned his sorrows, passes out on the steps of the Colliseum, and is robbed by Giorgio, but Hayes does not invest the incident with more than passing significance.

Indeed, to his credit, Hayes resists the obvious temptation to tie his stories too tightly to their frame. The trial of the Questore runs throughout the novel and the stories are interspersed with it and draw on it for their significance; but the problems of the separate characters are not simply explainable in terms of Fascist guilt. Clearly, Fascism is at the root of their troubles, but the characters are not plot- or theme-ridden; rather their stories are clarified by being placed in juxtaposition to the trial. Thus, the successful machinations of the Marchese are more bitterly ironic because of the trial. And ironic too, though in a somewhat different sense, are the moral sterility of Captain Pollard and the Allied government he represents, and the poignant search for love of Carla and Harry.

However, the theme of the novel *is* concerned with Fascist guilt. The story of the trial, told from the alternate points of view of the prosecution and the defense, focuses upon the question of the responsibility of the Questore for the slaughter of the innocents.

The Questore is a slow-witted, semi-articulate party hack who had risen slowly through the ranks to the position of enforcer. His defense is presented in a dream which he has on the night before sentence is to be handed down. In the dream, he can explain; in the dream, the court will wait and listen and perhaps understand, for there is no clever, sharp-tongued prosecutor present to deflate and destroy his testimony. The prosecution's case too is presented separately in the novel, before the dream sequence, in fact, in a long address by the Prosecutor. But the two sections complement each other exactly, and for purposes of this discussion, it would be well to merge or collate them.

The Questore's defense, in his dream, is that he had acted under orders, that he had been pressured by his reluctant superior to sign the death warrants, and that therefore he was not responsible. "That is how life is arranged", he argues; "there is a dynasty of superiors to whom one is answerable, who give the orders and accept the responsibility. That is how it must be." [6] "One has one's job, and besides, one has the authorization", is the Prosecutor's comment; "the wonderful absolution of authorization!" [7]

In order further to explain and to excuse his actions, the Questore characterizes himself as a not very intelligent or very gregarious person:

'Inside me there was this heaviness, this lack of something always. . . . It was not that I did not wish to respond; it was that I could not respond, ever. It was difficult for me to feel or to penetrate an existence that was not my own; a flower, an animal, another being. . . . So that I was alone inside my nature, always. . . . in the end, I accepted this separation of myself from the others.' [8]

He was loose, without human ties, without faith and with nothing he wished to hope for.

The Prosecutor agrees with this self-analysis: "His very defects as a human being contribute to his success as a fascist." [9] But he points out too, that not simply a psychological quirk or intellectual inadequacy had caused the birth and growth of Fascism (the Questore, like Pettinger, comes slowly to represent the party, not simply an individual member of it); environment too had played a major role. After the first World War, Italy was economically and socially depressed, and her citizens were restless for a change, for better times. Projecting backward, the Prose-

[6]   Hayes, *All Thy Conquests*, p. 198.
[7]   *Ibid.*, p. 108.
[8]   *Ibid.*, p. 198.
[9]   *Ibid.*, p. 108.

cutor sees that the ex-soldier misanthrope " 'is poor; he is dis-
couraged; he is bitter; he sleeps badly. He is ripe for politics' ".[10]
For much the same reasons, Pettinger had been equally ripe.

And the Questore corroborates the attachment to the party.
A man had been beaten in the piazza, he remembers in his dream,
and he was part of the crowd which wonders who had beaten
him, and why:

'In the war it had been different. In the war one assumed that others
were responsible: the king, the general staff, the mystical nation. The
dead in the moutains during the war were obviously not one's own
responsibility, and besides, one was always in the war so near death
oneself. It was only that soldiers did not like to see the man they
shot fall. The falling was for a brief moment uncomfortable. But in
the war it was different, and the responsibility was clearly theirs
during the war, but here, in the piazza, the responsibility was not yet
clear.' [11]

So, in answer to the restless grumbling of the crowd, an orator
steps forward to make it clear:

'They lived, he and the others, and the bleeding man, in a time of
great historical change. History, the orator wished them to understand,
was beyond good or evil, beyond scruples, beyond questions of conscience. The nation was the conscience. And since history, which
demands of us only the noblest of acts, the greatest of devotions, the
profoundest of loyalties, the most rigorous of disciplines, is born out
of violence, the Party (a noi! a noi!) itself, that great instrument of
history, would assume the responsibility.

'Violence, a bleeding man, was necessary. The necessity, and the
Party, absolved one.' [12]

Thus does Hayes portray the birth of Fascism; through the mind
and eyes of a sheep rather than a shepherd. The Questore is no
Pettinger, despite the parallels; he is more an effect than a cause.
But the Prosecutor argues that he must not be allowed to hide
behind this fact in order to escape responsibility for his crimes.
His stupidity, his poverty, his bitterness may not excuse him.
Nor may the authorization. The Prosecutor asks for the death
penalty:

[10]   *Ibid.*, p. 107.
[11]   *Ibid.*, p. 196.
[12]   *Ibid.*, p. 197.

'Twenty years, signori: twenty years we have endured these careers. Twenty years we have bled from such authorizations. O *youth youth,* they sang, *springtime of beauty!* But this is the harvest of their ages; from Istria to the Gulf our country lies irreparably ruined. And who knows what terrible surgery may be needed before we are healed? Who knows what medicine, bitterer than the illness, may be necessary before we are well again?' [13]

And at the end of his dream, in a superbly ironic passage, the Questore stands before the Pope at the gates of paradise:

And heaven opened: there, rank upon rank, with all their transfigured faces, stood the blessed armies of the subordinates, each forgiven identically, each washed clean of his sin, each at last having transferred the burden of his humanity to the Son, and each, while choirs sang and doves plunged through the humming air, celestially and eternally authorized.[14]

The only element not figured upon either by the prosecution or the defense is the people, those who had been misled, deluded, and finally disillusioned for twenty years by men like the Questore and their masters. Hayes introduces them as a cynical, disbelieving, mistrusting Chorus:

Who knows, perhaps they will acquit:
How can they acquit? How can they dare acquit?
He has too much money, says Paolo Benedetto,
who will begin driving a bus again for his old company as soon as the directors can find some tires. Besides, says Benedetto, they are all former fascists themselves. Which one of them, says Benedetto, has really clean hands? [15]

And neither the specious arguments of the Questore, nor the reassuring announcement of the Prosecutor in resisting the temptation to argue emotionally instead of rationally – " 'I will restrain myself, because in a time when justice is in disrepute and truth hardly believed in, I find myself oddly believing in justice and in truth!' " [16] – can prevent the explosion of the people into

---

[13]   *Ibid.*, p. 109.
[14]   *Ibid.*, p. 204.
[15]   *Ibid.*, p. 8.
[16]   *Ibid.*, p. 104.

violent action. They invade the court on the day that sentence is to be passed and drag the Questore away to retribution. A *nuncio* describes the scene to the Chorus:

'... the Court itself must have been in panic. For it was not what the magistrates had expected. This was to be a trial, carefully prepared for, carefully announced, of great political import and dignity: a calm dispensation of the law, a ceremony of witnesses and speeches, in which careers would be made and reputations enhanced, climaxed at last by a solemn sentence handed down by His Excellency, the Predent, and photographed by the newsreels. They had, all the distinguished gentlement of the Court, so carefully groomed themselves for this moment, and justice, in their hands, was to come forth, neatly packaged, tied with their little sanctioned bows. They would avenge the people, of course, for after all, they were the instruments of the people, but the people did not wait.' [17]

The people beat the Questore, stone him, and drop him from a bridge into the Tiber. A boat full of young men is rowed out, and they pound on the struggling victim until finally he sinks and drowns.

A closer analogy exists between the Questors and two relatively minor characters from *The Crusaders,* Heberle and Mulsinger. They are two German soldiers drafted for "Operation Buzzard", an elaborate plan to assassinate all Allied General officers dreamed up by Marshall Klemm-Borowski and put into effect by Pettinger. The plan is a resounding failure. Most of the assassins, including Heberle and Mulsinger, whose target was General Farrish, are discovered. And, because they are posing as American soldiers dressed in army uniforms, they are sentenced to die as spies before a firing squad.

Lt. Yates is given the job of making propaganda capital out of the situation. He interviews the condemned men, and hears them argue that the penalty is unjust:

'I don't want to die', Heberle said miserably.
'D'you think the man you went out to kill wanted to die?'
'But we didn't kill him!'
'Not because you didn't try!. ... And do you think that all the defenseless people that your Army, your SS, your Secret Police have killed in the course of this war, and still are killing, wanted to die?'

[17]   *Ibid.,* pp. 290-91.

'But I have nothing to do with that! Don't you see, sir – I only followed orders! I'm not responsible!' [18]

Yates, angry, and certain of the justice of his anger for the first time, dashes out at the complainants:

He said sharply, 'Let's get another thing straight, Heberle – and you, Mulsinger! The time has come when men have to stand up to the things they do. This hiding behind your superiors is no good any more – because, no doubt, they will hide behind their superiors, and so on up the line, until nobody is guilty but one man; until all the suffering of the war is atoned for by one bullet in that one man's brain. It's not going to work that way. If you have a heap of dung, the lowest layer stinks just as much, even though you take a shovelful off the top. You're going to be judged by what you, yourselves have done – every single one of you.' [19]

There is remarkable agreement among the novelists that such a blanket judgment of the Germans is justifiable if not necessary. There is only one Questore, whose guilt does not spread out to embrace Carla and Giorgio, though in a sense, his punishment does; but there are many Heberles and Mulsingers in the novels – physical enemies at least as dangerous as the Japanese, and ideological enemies far more dangerous than the Italians.

Lt. Stillman, in William Fridley's *A Time to go Home*, retreating from the Bulge battle with only some forty men left out of an entire infantry battalion,

now understood, what he could not have known before – that the Nazis were fighting fiercely and with courage and passion for their cause. They were not a bewildered mass praying for deliverance. There had been no black-clad SS troops standing behind those soldiers moving out across the valley today. Those green-clad troops were fighting for the base creed of the Nazis with ... intensity of conviction.[20]

And Lt. Garnett, in Ned Calmer's *The Strange Land*, whose company had come close to capture at the Bulge, reflects para-

---

[18] Heym, *The Crusaders*, p. 400. Walter Freeman, *The Last Blitzkrieg*, is a rather weak novel based upon the same incident. It is written from a screenplay of the same title.
[19] *Ibid.*, p. 401.
[20] William Fridley, *A Time to go Home*, p. 104.

noically on what might have been the results of such capture:

Right now the two Jews in my platoon would be headed for Dachau concentration camp. That's where they hang living men up by the collar bone on meat hooks. Or Belsen concentration camp. That's where they turn loose ravenous dogs on naked Jews to tear of their genitals. In Poland the Nazi exterminator squads throw little Jewish boys and girls into concrete mixers for a joke. At Ravensbrueck the women wardens whip the breasts of the most beautiful Jewish girls until there's nothing left but ribbons of flesh.[21]

The lengthy portrayals of the horrors of German concentration camps in *The Crusaders* and *The Young Lions* serve to extend this hateful fear of the military to the German people as a whole; for the people, Heym and Shaw make clear, knew of the existence of the camps and tolerated if not approved of them.

There are few attempts to excuse the Germans, individually or as a group, for the crimes of Nazism. There is none of the attitude prevalent among the World War I novelists that Germans are human beings, even as you and I; that they, as we, were duped by the munitions makers or war-mongering politicians; that they were guiltless tools in the hands of clever and unscrupulous militarists. There is instead the firm conviction that they all knew, like Pettinger, exactly where they were going, and how, and at what cost for whom. There are no Giulias, Giorgios or Carlas, or Lisas in the novels about Germany; the novelists are too aware of guilt and retribution to create them.[22] Stefan Heym gives us one of the few even moderately sympathetic

[21]   Ned Calmer, *The Strange Land*, p. 330.
[22]   The one novel which treats the Germans most compassionately is William Smith's *Last of the Conquerors*. It is a story about Negro occupation troops and their acceptance as equals by the German people though they are discriminated against within the army. But Smith is concerned not so much with absolving Germans of their guilt for the war, nor with praising them as tolerant and enlightened, as with condemning Americans for their unenlightened intolerance. John Killens' *And Then We Heard the Thunder*, a novel dealt with at length in the next chapter, treats the same subject in the Pacific Theater.
    American concern with German guilt and responsibility was not confined to the novelists, of course. According to Oscar T. Barck, Jr. (*A History of the United States Since 1945*, pp. 18-19) more than 835,000 were brought into court at Nuremburg, and of these, some 518,400 were found guilty of some form of war crime.

portrayals in his characterization of the courageous widow of Ensdorf, Frau Petrik, who tries in vain to save the people trapped in the abandoned mine by Pettinger's scorched-earth policy. But she and her fellow townspeople serve chiefly to delineate the conscious and unconscious brutality of Pettinger and Dondolo; except for Frau Petrik, whose fear is as strong as her courage, they are all simple victims.

Edward Loomis in *End of a War* considers with great care the difficulty of treating even non-Nazi, non-military Germans like Frau Petrik sympathetically or with compassion. The hero of the novel, George Leggett, is an American infantryman who has been an exceptionally good soldier-killer. At the war's end, with the cessation of excitement and danger and the restoration of a certain amount of normality to his life, Leggett finds himself uneasy about the killing he has done and about his satisfaction at having done it. The uneasiness becomes guilt very rapidly, depressing him terribly, and making expiation mandatory to restore his peace of mind. He is in Germany at the time, and he makes himself the protector of a German family, the Hesses, which had been dispossessed by the war. He feeds them, gets fuel for them, moves them with him when he is transferred. But nothing seems to work; his depression deepens.

Part of the problem is that the Hesses accept his kindness to them as their due. They are unaware of any responsibility and guilt of their own for the war and its consequences. Leggett's is a one-way expiation, and it is unsatisfactory because he knows the guilt is not his alone while his equally guilty confessors assume that it is. As a case in point, Leggett is assigned to guard a Displaced Persons camp, the majority of whose inmates had been liberated from German concentration camps. Reminiscent of Sgt. Bing in *The Crusaders*, he becomes extremely upset over the plight of these people and over the fact that they cannot be freed because their liberators have not arranged for someplace for them to go. They are still caged, though technically free. Leggett explains his feelings to the Hesses, who, after all, as Germans, had been the original offenders of these people. He feels they should sympathize, but they hardly even understand.

" 'But there are bad people in the camps!' " Chrystel tells him. " 'They would not be in the camps, behind the barbed wire, if they were not bad people. And many Germans have been killed by them; this we know, George; we have heard it from many families already!' " [23]

Profoundly shocked by this attitude, Leggett nonetheless clings to the Hesse family as the only means of salvation from his guilt and its consequent depression. Finally, in a burst of expiatory eloquence, he confesses all to them – his joy in killing, his pleasure in seeing German corpses as the army advanced, and knowing that he had been responsible for some of them. And he tries to describe for them too how the guilt descended upon him with the end of the war. But the Hesses turn from him in fright; not only do they not understand and forgive him, thereby meriting his understanding and forgiveness – they reject him as a monster, fearfully, even scornfully.

The novel ends with Leggett's existential realization that only he is capable of forgiving himself; that even if the Hesses had absolved him, he still would have had to suffer the "private consequences" of his sin. But the first large push toward this realization is given Leggett by the Hesses, who reveal the base nature and motives of the German people. The Hesses assuredly are not villains; but just as certainly, they are not the innocents that Leggett had led himself to believe they were at the outset.

Though the novelists found it difficult to be sympathetic or even objective about any German, it was the Nazi, particularly, as we have seen, the Nazi military which they considered most dangerous and insidious. And, along with *The Crusaders*, the novel which most clearly delineates this danger is Irwin Shaw's *The Young Lions*.

This is a story of the war in the European Theatre from Africa through the fall of Germany. It is told from the points of view of three soldiers: Michael Whitaker, a disenchanted American liberal who gradually recovers his idealism; Noah Ackerman an American Jew who wages a courageous battle against anti-semitism among Americans, thereby leading Whitaker toward

---

[23]   Edward Loomis, *End of a War*, p. 214.

commitment; and Christian Diestl, a Wehrmacht sergeant who follows a path almost exactly opposite to Whitaker's, traveling downward from an idealistic commitment to social reform to hardcore Nazism.

In his conception and portrayal of Diestl, Shaw does something unique to the war novels: he develops a villain, allowing him to grow and become. He does not assume our preconceptions concerning Nazism and build upon the assumptions; he gives us Christian Diestl as a man, and allows us to watch him degenerate – largely through the influence of his ideological mentor, the Nazi, Lt. Hardenburg – into an animal who betrays comradeship in the name of a cause he knows is lost, and who kills simply for the sake of killing.

At the outset of the novel, Margaret Fremantle, a young American woman on a skiing vacation in the Austrian Alps, is nearly raped by a drunken German servant at the inn. The next day she complains to Diestl, at this time a ski-instructor, that to her mind, the German's action was "all of a piece" with Nazism. After a moment of anger, Diestl answers that " 'Frederick did not climb into your room because he was a Nazi. . . . Frederick did that because he is a pig. He's a bad human being. For him it is only an accident that he is a Nazi. Finally, if it comes to it, he will be a bad Nazi, too.' " [24]

Then, very patiently, he explains to Margaret why he believes in Nazism, and why he feels that Nazism is the only answer for a troubled Europe. Communism is too reasonable; " 'In Europe nothing will ever be accomplished by reason.' " Brotherhood is nonsense; lying, murdering, cheating are the only things that Europeans understand. However, Diestl's social idealism shines through this realistic appraisal:

'Do you think I like to say that? But it is true, and only a fool will think otherwise. Then, finally, when things are in order, we can stop what you call the "lying and murdering". When people have enough to eat, when they have jobs, when they know that their money will be worth the same tomorrow as it is today and not one-tenth as much, when they know they have a government that is their own, that cannot be ordered around by anyone else, at anyone else's whim . . . when they can stop being defeated. Out of weakness, you get nothing. Shame, starvation. That's all. Out of strength, you get everything.' [25]

But his amorality, his belief in expediency, the seeds of his later viciousness are present in these final words:

'And about the Jews . . .' He shrugged. 'It is an unlucky accident. Somehow, someone discovered that that was the only way to come to power. I am not saying I like it. Myself, I know it is ridiculous to attack any race. Myself, I know there are Jews like Frederick, and Jews, say, like myself. But if the only way you can get a decent and ordered Europe is by wiping out the Jews, then we must do it. A little injustice for a large justice. It is the one thing the Comrades have taught Europe – the end justifies the means. It is a hard thing to learn, but, finally, I think, even Americans will learn it.' [26]

At the fall of Paris, Diestl, by now a Wehrmacht sergeant, is still idealistic enough to look optimistically toward future days "because they were going to be peaceful and rich, and all the ideas for which he had been willing to risk his life would be put into law and made permanent and a new time of prosperity and order was beginning".[27]

But Diest's idealistic hopes are gradually undermined during the next few months. He is given the unpleasant duty, for a soldier, of working with collaborators to break up incipient underground movements and to arrest hiding Jews. He discovers that most of his comrades, and most of his officers, are operating in the black market. Even the most basic morality seems to be at a premium.

At this point, Diestl receives leave, and travels hopefully back to Germany, to an energetic world without hypocrisy or phoniness. But he has been asked by Lt. Hardenburg to deliver a gift to Gretchen, his wife, in Berlin, and he discovers a sort of Roman corruption in the new capital of Europe that lay unsuspected beneath a facade of dignity and ceremony. Gretchen does an important job in the Ministry of Propaganda trying to convince German girls that it is unpatriotic to consort with the foreign

[25] *Ibid.*, p. 19.
[26] *Ibid.*, p. 20.
[27] *Ibid.*, p. 91.

slave laborers who have been imported into the country. She herself is a favorite of the members of the General Staff, and is paid for her services in favors and in loot from defeated countries. She seduces Christian on the very first day they meet, and convinces him with a minimum of effort to spend his entire leave in Berlin, waiting for her call for service. But Gretchen is more than sexually competent and sexually hungry; she is also sexually jaded. She returns to Christian one evening with a Lesbian friend, and the three of them engage in a tumultuous orgy.

Revolted, yet terribly attracted by the uninhibited evil of Gretchen, and by his own newly discovered evil potential, Christian allows her to use her influence in an attempt to have him commissioned and transferred to Berlin, attached to the General Staff. With few pangs of conscience, Christian is willing to sacrifice his desire to be an active part in world reform in order to remain an active part of corruption. And this willingness leaves him considerably emptier when, because he had once been a communist, his commission and transfer are denied him. The crowning blow comes when Gretchen rejects him for the same reasons; he has become a danger to her position in the government.

Bitter, considerably less the idealist, Diestl returns to France, resolved to get his share of black market wealth, knowing that with it he can buy Gertchen's favor in spite of the danger involved. But even this satisfaction is denied him, for while he was on leave, his outfit was alerted to move into combat with Rommel.

While in Africa, the badly shaken foundations of Diestl's convictions are utterly destroyed. Under orders, he takes part in the cold-blooded massacre of an English patrol – the glory of war is denied him; still under orders, he retreats with Lt. Hardenburg, leaving the balance of the company behind to defend a defenseless position – he rejects and betrays comradeship. Finally, the convoy to which he and the lieutenant have attached themselves in retreat is bombed by American planes, so that both men wind up in hospitals on Capri – he tastes defeat.

Thus is Diestl brought to the brink of that total disillusionment which Remarque's German soldiers reached at the moment of imminent defeat in *All Quiet on the Western Front*. He is rescued by the realization that, while Africa might be lost, the balance of the New Germany remained intact; and by the lessons taught him in the sickroom of Lt. Hardenburg, "a combination of lecture room and confessional, a place in which Christian could find his own mistakes clarified, his own vague hopes and aspirations crystallized, understood, categorized".[28] His mistake had been his idealism; his vague hope had been for power at any cost.

Lt. Hardenburg, masochist (he had asked to be flagellated by a French whore on his first night in Paris), sadist (humming tunelessly, he had waited to open fire on the English patrol in Africa until most of them were squatting at their latrine), grotesque (his face had been destroyed in the bombing), devotes himself wholeheartedly to the education of his sergeant. He gives Christian no new idealism, nor even attempts to shore up the old. He gives him instead the hard, practical facts of Nazi-Fascism.

Lying in his hospital bed, his face hidden in bandages, the room steeped in the odor of its other patient – a mummy-swathed, moaning figure identified only as The Burn – Hardenburg lectures to the visiting Diestl:

'After this one is over, we must leap into another war. Against the Japanese. It is always necessary to subdue your allies. It is something that is left out of *Mein Kampf*, perhaps out of shrewdness on the author's part. And after that, it will be necessary to permit some nation, somewhere, to grow strong, so that we can always have an enemy who will be difficult to beat. To be great, a nation must always be stretched to the limits of its endurance. . . . It is never possible to enjoy the fruits of war in peace. The fruits of war can only be enjoyed in further war, or you lose everything. . . .

'We Germans have the best chance of all. We have an elite of daring and intelligent men, and we have a large, energetic population. It is true that other nations, say the Americans, have as many daring and intelligent men, and a population that is at least as energetic. But we are more fortunate, for one reason, and we shall conquer because of it. We are docile and they are not and probably never will be.' [29]

28   *Ibid.*, p. 287.
29   *Ibid.*, pp. 288-89.

He goes on to speak of his wound, of the fact that it can be turned to his advantage after the war if he enters politics – it will be his badge of honor, his medal. The horror of it, he is convinced, will not repel him; the soldier lives on horror, on death and the threat of death. Hardenburg expands this theme:

'For the purpose of our country we need an empty Europe. It is a mathematical problem and the equalizing sign in slaughter. . . .

'Wherever we go everyone must realize that we are quick to kill. It is the most satisfactory key to dominion. Eventually I came to enjoy killing, as a pianist enjoys the Czerny which keeps his fingers limber for the Beethoven.' [30]

He upbraids Diestl for feeling optimistic about the end of the war and the coming of peace and prosperity:

'We can be prosperous only if all Europe is a pauper. . . . Do I want the illiterate Pole, drunk on potato alcohol in the winter mud of his village, to be prosperous? Do I want the stinking goatherd in the Dolomites to be rich? Do I want a fat Greek homosexual to teach Law at Heidelberg? Why? I want servants, not competitors. And failing that, I want corpses.' [31]

Uncompromising brutality and viciousness are absolutely essential to victory. Hardenburg proposes that Germany should kill one hundred thousand Europeans ("'And not Jews, because everyone is used to seeing Jews killed and everyone is more or less secretly delighted with our efficiency in that field'") for every day that the war continues, and should drop their names and photographs over London instead of bombs. "'Killing is an objective act and death is a state beyond right and wrong.'" [32]

Pure logic, sweet reasonableness, and a willingness to deviate from the rules – these are the ingredients of victory and power. They are abnormalities, and are the causes and effects of further abnormalities. But to Hardenburg's mind, the abnormal is essential:

'The German soldier has the good luck that at this balancing moment

[30] *Ibid.*, p. 290.
[31] *Ibid.*, p. 291.
[32] *Ibid.*, p. 292.

in history he is being led by men who are a little mad. Hitler falls into fits before the maps at Berchtesgaden. Goering was dragged from the sanitarium for dope addicts in Sweden. Roehm, Rosenberg, all the rest, would make old Dr. Freud rub his hands in Vienna if he peeked out and saw them waiting in his anteroom. Only the irrational vision of a madman could understand that an empire could be won in ten years merely by promising to institutinalize the pogrom ... We are being led against the sane and reasonable armies of men who could not deviate from the rules if they burst a kidney in the effort, and we are being led by men exalted by opium fumes and by gibbering Corporals who picked up their lessons in military affairs from serving tea in a trench to a broken Captain twent-five years ago at Passchendaele. How can we expect to lose?' [33]

So end Hardenburg's lectures to Diestl, and, as if to punctuate them finally, Hardenburg has Christian smuggle a bayonet to him so that he can put The Burn out of his misery. Diestl complies, then limps away from the room on his shattered knee, going back into action, feeling "like a scholar who has finally been graduated from a university whose every book he has memorized and sucked dry".[34]

Lt. Hardenburg is Shaw's symbol, his personified definition, of Nazi-Fascism. Because he recognizes and is willing to utilize abnormality, because he is openly, expediently, amoral, Harden‑ burg is potentially more dangerous even than Hitler. But Nazism is defeated in the end, and Shaw carries the symbol to its logical conclusion: rejected by Gretchen when he expresses a desire to return to her, Hardenburg commits suicide with a pen-knife.

Gretchen too is a significant symbol. When, after front-line duty in Italy, Christian returns on leave once more to Berlin, he finds her to be no longer a glamorous woman doing a glamorous job in a glamorous society. She has become the lover of a French Lesbian who keeps her carefully locked away from men. Gretchen is the New Germany, slowly retreating, slowly being destroyed both from within and from without. She is defeat; she is the land to which the maimed and humiliated German army must return. And in her selfishness, she rejects her responsibility for that army: " 'You people are getting queerer and queerer these

[33]   *Ibid.*, p. 293.
[34]   *Ibid.*, p. 297.

days. . . . Sometimes I have the feeling you all ought to be locked up, really I do.' " [35] She tells Christian that Hardenburg had sent her a photograph of his disfigured face and asked to return to her. After she had refused, as tactfully as possible, he killed himself.

Diestl by this time has become so hardened, so almost monomaniacal in his acceptance of Nazism, that the corruption of Gretchen and the suicide of Hardenburg only make him more stubbornly loyal to a losing cause. There seems to be a rather serious weakness in characterization here. Christian is hardly moved, and his faith is never shaken, by news of Hardenburg's death. Granted that the destruction of his illusions and ideals coupled with the Lieutenant's lectures effectively have made him more a machine and less a man than he was before, it still seems reasonable to suppose that Hardenburg's suicide should shock him back to humanity, if only for a moment. Still, he is consistent, and, if such a thing is possible, he becomes even more consistent throughout the remainder of the novel.

He is given one final opportunity to regain his humanity. Retreating, his outfit wiped out, Diestl meets Brandt, an artist, an old friend and ex-comrade. Brandt has an automobile, and he convinces Christian to consider deserting. They motor to Paris, and move into the house of Brandt's French fiancee, Simone. Christian and Brandt had known Simone five years before, at the fall of Paris; Brandt had remained in Paris when Christian had moved to Rennes. There had been another girl, Francoise, and thought they had dated, Christian had never been allowed to make love to her. Francoise shares Simone's house, and because " 'You're very tired now. . . . A little gray. And I notice that you limp a bit, too. In '40 it did not seem you could ever grow tired. You might die, then, I thought, in one glorious burst of fire, but never weary, never . . . ' " [36] because "You're not a conqueror anymore, darling, you're a refugee . . .' " [37] she now gives herself to Christian.

[35] *Ibid.*, p. 426.
[36] *Ibid.*, p. 576.
[37] *Ibid.*, p. 578.

The chance for redemption through humility is given him, but
Diestl rejects it:

Better friends than Brandt had died beside him for four years; should
Brandt be left alive to suck on Hardenburg's bones? Then end justified
the means – and after the geometric slaughter, was the end to be
civilian Brandt, after three or four easy months is an American stock-
ade, returning to his soft French wife, painting his silly, piddling pictures, apologizing for the next twenty years to the victors for the hard,
dead men he had betrayed? [38]

The answers are obvious; Diestl steals out of the house and goes
directly to the SS. He even accompanies them to make the arrest.

The balance of Diestl's story is anti-climactic. In an attempt
to reach the German lines, he is trapped in a woods near the
concentration camp which the American Company that Whitaker
and Ackerman belong to have liberated. In a futile, senseless
gesture, Diestl kills Ackerman from ambush and is hunted down
and killed by Whitaker. The symbolic significance of the fact
that Ackerman is a Jew is underscored by the fact that Diestl
does not know this when he fires; the death of Ackerman, the
whole Jewish persecution, was simply an accident of history. It
was the result of a belief in the simple, single solution, in expedient, capricious action; it was the result of a whole way of
thinking and living which, spawned by and living on death, had
to end in death as well. The whole final scene of the novel calls
to mind Brandt's prophecy made before Christian betrayed him:

'Maybe, somewhere, they'll collect some troops and draw a line, but
it will only be a gesture. A temporary, blood-thirsty gesture. A sick,
romantic Viking funeral. Clausewitz and Wagner, the General Staff
and Siegfried, combined for a graveyard theatrical effect.' [39]

In spite of the slickness of the novel's execution, a slickness
which allows the plot to take command of the character on occa-
sion, and permits the dialogue to lapse into essay form – in spite
of the overwhelming coincidence which brings its three soldiers
together to perform a perfect, hence somewhat unconvincing
climax – *The Young Lions* remains a serious, carefully done

[38]   *Ibid.*, p. 579.
[39]   *Ibid.*, p. 563.

novel of ideas. It is not as good a book as *The Crusaders* or *All Thy Conquests,* but it is as convincing a book. Christian Diestl, like Col. Pettinger and the Questore, comes successfully to represent the first face of that physical and ideological evil which the war novelists hated and sought to destroy.

IV. THE SECOND FACE OF VILLAINY

The second face of villainy drawn by the novelists is more familiar and recognizable than the first. It is an American face, the face of Lt. Col. Willoughby and Mess Sgt. Dondolo. Nazi-Fascism is, for the novelists, the epitome of all that is morally and ethically evil: it justifies amoral means by materialistic ends; it permits the individual to reject responsibility for his actions though he may with impunity enjoy the fruits of them; it sub-scribes to the simple, single solution to physical and philosophical problems – to racism, concentration camps, and mass murder. The novelists believe that anything or anyone which reflects these aspects of Fascism, even in part, is potentially as evil. They believe that in the presence of parts of the definition is contained the immanence of the whole; that the tendency toward evil casts the shadow of its epitome.

They found the tendency within many Americans – within 100% Americanism, within the businessman's morality, within that complacency which encourages a world view based on good guys vs. bad guys, and which results so often in an aggressive paranoia, and within that other kind of complacency which recognizes the tendencies and contrives to use them to further its own ends.

For most of the novelists, the danger of this tendency toward evil among Americans was as great as Nazi-Fascism, the evil itself. America was on the winning side in the war. The first face of villainy – Pettinger, the Questore, Hardenburg, Diestl – could and would be destroyed. But the destruction of them, ironically, might justify the existence of the second face. Success does not shake the confidence of the complacent; rather it entrenches it, feeds it, and even gives it weapons. Thus, the novelists reserve their most withering attacks for the second face, and they couple the attacks with a solemn warning, a fearful prophecy. Willoughby and Dondolo for instance clearly represent the two major facets of Fascism: its materialistic expediency and its brutality. They are each discredited, defeated, cast out; but each ends better off than when he began. Dondolo has his black market profits and he is removed from front line duty; Willoughby has his cartel and an assured successful future in his law firm. Their danger, their villainy, is greater at the war's end than it was at its start; it is greater after the death of Pettinger and the collapse of Nazism than it was before or during the crusade against them.

Few of the novelists constructed such pointed or extended analogies between the two faces of villainy as Stefan Heym. Many of them simply took broad, all encompassing swipes at every unpleasant or dishonest aspect of America or Americanism without really pinning the fascist label upon any of them.

Into this category fall Anton Myrer's *The Big War* and John Horne Burns' *The Gallery*. Each of these novelists editorially whips 100% Americanism almost until it bleeds. Each of them argues that much of the guilt for the war rests with America, as does even more of the responsibility for the peace. And significantly, each of them makes the argument stick.

Alan Newcombe, the intellectual spokesman for author Myrer in *The Big War,* points out that Americans

... had been reared incorrectly ... they had been brought up to believe that life was easy and good, that possessions and vitamins were the unfailing buttress against ill fortune (for ill fortune did not need to happen really, it was somehow or other only the result of carelessness or self-destructive impulses, a consequence of some inherent weakness that good people – really *good people* – never permitted to take root): that they were, in short, Americans – the privileged ones of this earth, endowed with good clothing and good teeth, with destinies sure and sound as the orbit of the moon. The handsome young boy always got the beautiful young girl. The concept of disaster, of an implacable, hostile fate, of a life swept irreparably away from comfort or superiority or even individual identity – such a concept never penetrated their minds; it was not consonant with tile bathrooms and tweed jackets and built-in cabinets, all the good things of this world . . .

They had lost that, he saw with sudden burnished clarity; and for this dereliction they had paid – as he himself had – with a terrible estrangement from the rest of the world — an alienation they dimly sensed and which had filled them with a peculiar raging dissatisfaction. And so they had seized on the false trappings, the old economic superiority, had clung to it, flung it riotously in each others' faces, in fevered pride climbed out of bulbous flashing cars and thrown open the doors of extravagant mansions, thrown half-dollars from the rails of liners to dripping drivers, chucked the chins of brown-skinned children in picturesque streets, whipped out fantastically expensive cameras and snapped and snapped and snapped – all to veil from themselves their sense of self-repugnance, their guilt, their isolate despair. . . .[1]

Here, in the constitutional inability of Americans to face themselves and the world clearly and straight, Myrer is saying; in their tendency to substitute materialistic superficialities for values, rests an ever-present danger to peace. The Japanese are evil, and certainly, a war against such evil, a war to "comfort man where he is in misery", is justified. But much of the guilt for war must be assumed by shortsighted, complacent Americans.

This conclusion is reinforced in Burns' *The Gallery,* primarily in the "Portrait" of Hal and in certain of the introspective, first-person sections of the novel called "Promenades". Consider this passage from the "Third Promenade": "There was something abroad which we Americans couldn't or wouldn't understand. But unless we made some attempt to realize that everyone in the world isn't American, and that not everything American is good, we'd all perish together, and in this twentieth century. . . . "[2] Or consider these editorial snatches from the "Seventh Promenade":

I found that outside of the propaganda writers (who were making a handsome living from the deal) Americans were very poor spiritually. Their ideals were something to make dollars on. They had bankrupt souls. . . .

Our propaganda did everything but tell us Americans the truth: that we had most of the riches of the modern world, but very little of its

---

[1]   Myrer, *The Big War,* p. 392.
[2]   Burns, *The Gallery,* p. 97.

soul. We were nice enough guys in our own country, most of us; but when we got overseas, we could not resist the temptation to turn a dollar or two at the expense of the people who were already down.. I can speak only of Italy, for I didn't see France or Germany. But with our Hollywood ethics and our radio network reasoning we didn't take the trouble to think out the fact that the war was supposed to be against fascism – not against every man, woman, and child in Italy. . . . But then a modern war is total. Armies on the battlefield are simply a remnant from the old kind of war. In the 1944 war everyone's hand ended by being against everyone else's. Civilization was already dead, but nobody bothered to admit this to himself.[3]

Then, becoming more specific, Burns comments on black marketing and related evils:

I remember that there were not a few really big criminals who stole stuff off the ships unloading in Naples harbor, stuff that didn't belong to them by *any* stretch of the imagination. For all this that I saw I could only attribute a deficient moral and humane sense to Americans as a nation and as a people . . . I saw that we could mouth democratic catchwords and yet give the Neapolitans a huge black market. I saw that we could prate of the evils of Fascism, yet be just as ruthless as Fascists with people who'd already been pushed into the ground. . . . The arguments that we advanced to cover our delinquencies were as childishly ingenuous as American advertising.[4]

These excerpts recall the words of Antonio, an anti-Fascist Italian ex-soldier, addressed to Robert in Alfred Hayes' *Girl on the Via Flaminea*:

'When we go into the street . . . what do we see? Your colonels, in their bigs cars, driving with women whose reputations were made in the bedrooms of fascist bureaucrats! With my country's enemies! Or your soldiers, drunk in our gutters. Or your officers, pushing us off our own sidewalks! Oh, the magnificent promises the radio made us! Oh, the paradise we'd have! Wait, wait – there will be bread, peace, freedom when the allies come! But where is this paradise?'[5]

Where, indeed? Both Hayes and Burns feel that it can never be realized as long as Americans remain peculiarly American. Burns makes this most articulately clear in his "Portrait" of Hal –

---

[3] *Ibid.*, pp. 259-60.
[4] *Ibid.*, p. 261.
[5] Hayes, *The Girl on the Via Flaminea*, p. 109.

clearly the best of the portraits in the novel because in it, Burns has managed to rein in his sentimentalism. Hal is an extremely sensitive, young American officer whose attempts to square his pacifist convictions with the necessity of the war, complicated by his attempts to understand the conflicting forces in his own nature – forces which include impotence and latent homosexuality – lead him finally to a megalomania in which he conceives of himself as Jesus Christ. And in the process, Hal's mind plays strange tricks; all of his repressed anger pours forth in a figment of his imaginations: the ghost of an ex-Broadway chorus-boy paratroop Captain who had been killed in Sicily. The vision appears to Hal in a bar in the Galleria, and it speaks Hal's repressed thoughts concerning Americans freely and openly. One passage in particular is worth quoting at length:

– You don't like Americans? Hal said. . . .

– Who does, except themselves? Automatons from the world's greatest factory. . . . They have no souls, you see . . . only the ability to add up to one million. Did you every hear them try to carry on a sensible conversation? . . . Oh, they've got quite an ingenious system of government, I grant you. But none of them gives a damn about it except when it gets them into a war. . . . They've got less maturity or individuality than any other peoples in the world. Poetry and Music to them-why they're deaf to anything that isn't sold by an advertising agency. . . . They don't know how to treat other human beings. With all their screaming about democracy, none of them has the remotest conception of human dignity. . . . Listen to the sounds that Negro band is making. That's their American music. Sexual moans and thumps . . . They don't know how to make love to a woman, and all their hatreds are between football teams or states of the same Union or for people they don't understand. Victims of the mob spirit and regimentation. . . . They've never really suffered. But when they get the first twinge of toothache of the soul, they start feeling sorry for themselves instead of learning any wisdom from pain.

– You're talking treason, Hal said. . . .

– Truth is always treasonous, the captain said, clicking his glass with a soft ferocity on the bar. And now these poor dears are involved in a war. This war is simply the largest mass murder in history. Theirs is the only country that has enough food and gasoline and raw materials. So they're expending these like mad to wipe out the others in the world who'd like a cut of their riches. In order to preserve their standard of living for a few more years, they've dreamed up ideologies. Or their big business has. So they're at war with nearly everybody else in the world. The rest of the world hates Americans because they're so crude and stupid and unimaginative ... They will win this war. They'll reduce Europe to a state of fifteen hundred years ago. Then their businessmen and their alphabetical bureaucracies will go into the shambles of Milan, Berlin, and Tokyo and open up new plants. ... International carpetbaggers. ... Millions of human beings will be dead, and most of the human feelings will be dead forever. ... Hurray for our side. ... We're destroying all the new ideas and all the little men of the world to make way for our mass production and our mass thinking and our mass entertainment. Then we can go back to our United States, that green little island in the midst of a smoking world. Then we can kill all the Negroes and the Jews. Then we'll start on Russia.[6]

The primary trouble with American and Americans as Myrer and Burns see it, is Americanism: a way of thought and action materialistically oriented and pragmatically justified. That Myrer and Burns did not push their thinking to the extreme that Heym does, and equate Americanism with Fascism, makes very little difference. The point is that all three of these novelists knew the enemy to be not merely physical but ideological as well; and not merely German and Italian and Japanese therefore, but American as well. That the ideology was on the one hand unformed and inchoate and on the other fully developed only made the evil of it that much more dangerous.

Others of the novelists pointed up certain superficial similarities between Fascism and Americanism without pushing them to analogical extremes. Irwin Shaw creates an entire Company of American anti-semites in *The Young Lions,* typified by Sgt. Rickett, a lisping Southerner who says to Noah Ackerman: " 'Ah'll tell yuh, heah an' now. Ah ain't got no use for Niggerth, Jewth, Mexicans or Chinamen, an' from now on you're goin' to have a powerful tough row to hoe in this here company. ... Now get your ass inside and keep it there. ... Move, Ikie, Ah'm tahd of lookin' at your ugly face.' "[7] The persistence of this

[6] *The Gallery*, pp. 75-76. The ellipses and hyphens are Burns'.
[7] Shaw, *The Young Lions*, p. 302.

attitude in the Company, coupled with a severe beating administered to him anonymously in the darkened Company street, prompts Noah to issue a vainglorious challenge to fight each of the men one at a time. He loses every fight but one, then he deserts, and upon his capture he is placed under psychiatric care. Eventually he wins the right to his self-respect and dignity, but at the expense of a badly battered body and mind — and at the expense of his life as well, for at the moment when he finally achieves selfhood, Christian Diestl pulls the trigger.

General Mallon in Ned Calmer's *The Strange Land,* a novel built around the Ardennes counter offensive, mentally labels a war correspondent named Marks, "Jew-Boy" and "Jew-Red", and calls his newspaper a " 'red rag' ".[8] And John C. Wexel, a syndicated human-interest columnist turned correspondent in the same novel is both anti-semitic and anti-Negro:

Maybe you can't expect to see much cooperation from soldiers commanded by a Jew. Garnett looks Jewish. He could be one of them who's changed his name. No matter how much these liberals . . . would deny it, the hatred exists. It's buried deep down. We have our American system of fair play, yes. But in the crisis hatred comes to the surface. That's when we show it. Garnett's men may feel it without knowing what it is. I couldn't blame them. It's almost as bad as expecting white men to be led into battle by a Negro. It won't work, that's all. Hitler knows that. It's one of the things he's right about.[9]

Unfortunately, such quick and superficial portrayals of American Fascism are not often integral to the novels in which they appear. They are fed in by the novelist because he cannot resist the opportunity to make the point, and as a consequence, they are often a bit too pat and perfect and one-dimensional. This is the case in *The Strange Land*. Wexel never really becomes a character in the novel, despite the fact that we read his thoughts extensively; he remains a simple testimonial to Calmer's hatred of Fascism. The same criticism must be made of the characterization of the paranoic executive officer in Martin Dibner's *The Deep Six* who asserts that "tyranny and fear breed the highest

8 Ned Calmer, *The Strange Land,* p. 73.
9 *Ibid.,* p. 229. Incidentally, Lt. Garnett is *not* Jewish.

form of efficiency man has ever known",[10] and about whom Lt. Austen, the hero of the novel, thinks: "Strange, to find the enemy here. Right in the goddamned pilot house." [11]

Despite the exaggeration in the episode from *The Young Lions,* the same criticism does not really apply to it; nor does it apply to the portrayal of Dondolo as anti-semitic in *The Crusaders.* In both of these instances, the situations *are* integral, for the character of Noah Ackerman is shaped in large part out of his traumatic experience in the Company, and Dondolo functions, as pointed out above, as one half of Pettinger's American alter ego, with Willoughby as the other half.

Norman Mailer and John O. Killens are the two authors other than Stefan Heym who construct most effectively a direct analogy between Americanism and Fascism. In fact, they both go much further than Heym: *The Naked and the Dead* and *And Then We Heard the Thunder* are both straight ideological anti-Fascist novels in which all of the Fascist villains are Americans. Part of the reason for this, of course, is that the Pacific war novelist lacked the opportunity which Heym had to include actual enemy Fascists in his novel. The Japanese, as noted earlier, were not ideological enemies as the Germans and Italians were; to hang on them the Fascist label would have been to misrepresent the nature of the war against them. Thus, in order to create believable villains, the novelists had to turn to Americans who were either actually or incipiently Fascistic. But in the case of Mailer and Killens, this is only a minor part of the reason. Both of these writers clearly wanted to portray and attack American Fascism and Fascists; there is every reason to suspect that, had their novels been set in Europe, the major villains would still have been American. German and Italian Nazi-Fascism was an accepted, agreed-upon evil. The real ideological danger lay in American tendencies toward the evil, and it is these tendencies that Mailer and Killens – and Heym – are most seriously concerned with. Their novels, from this point of view, are exposures and prophecies.

[10] Martin Dibner, *The Deep Six,* p. 213.
[11] *Ibid.,* p. 214.

Artistic dangers abound in such a situation. Anton Myrer mitigates them by concentrating his attack on Americanism generally. Martin Dibner falls victim in his abortive attempt to tie Japan and the Western world together ideologically through his exaggerated portrayal of the Fascistic executive officer of the *Atlantis* who, at the novel's climax, commits hara-kiri.[12] Mailer and Killens meet squarely every danger – exaggerated characterization, doubtful or too simple motivation, the tendency to editorialize – which faced the ideological novelist of the Pacific; and by a combination of sheer writing ability and great sincerity (and, in Killens' case particularly, tremendous subject matter) manage to pull free of nearly all of them.

The Naked and the Dead is the story of the successful attempt to re-take an island in the Pacific named Anopopei; Maj. Gen. George E. Cummings is in command of the campaign. The story is told on two levels; on one, the physical, with a substantial amount of the ideological mixed in, we follow the enlisted men of a reconnaissance platoon from shipboard through the invasion and many skirmishes, to the conclusion of the battle. On the other level, almost purely ideological, we are given the well-organized, carefully reasoned thoughts of General Cummings as he expresses them to his aide, Lt. Robert Hearn, a right-thinking though ineffectual liberal who stands at once as an exciting challenge to Cummings' intellectual position and as a straightman for his sophistries.

From the outset of the novel, Cummings works to educate and convert Hearn. The situation is somewhat similar to the relationship between Diestl and Hardenburg in *The Young Lions*, with the important difference that Hardenburg has a receptive and responsive pupil while Hearn stubbornly quarrels with the General's ideas and tactics. But Hearn's arguments have neither the strength nor the self-assurance of Cummings'. The General has thought his way carefully to his conclusions and beliefs; Hearn is literally feeling his way. " 'The root of the liberals' ineffectiveness comes right spang out of the desperate suspension in which they have to hold their minds' ", Cummings tells Hearn: " 'If you

[12]   *Ibid.*, pp. 262-64.

ever followed anything through to the end, not one of your ideas would last for an instant.' " [13]

These sentences are part of one of the two major exchanges between Cummings and Hearn. It has been precipitated by Hearn's protests that the enlisted men had not received their share of meat while the officers had received more than their share. The General justifies the situation in terms of a power philosophy:

'We have the highest standard of living in the world and, as one would expect, the worst individual fighting soldiers of any big power. . . . They're comparatively wealthy, they're spoiled, and as Americans they share most of them the peculiar manifestation of our democracy. They have an exaggerated idea of the rights due themselves as individuals and no idea at all of the rights due others. It's the reverse of the peasant, and I'll tell you right now it's the peasant who makes the soldiers.'

'So what you've got to do is break them down', Hearn said.

'Exactly. Break them down. Every time an enlisted man sees an officer get an extra privilege, it breaks him down a little more.'

'I don't see that. It seems to me they'd hate you more.'

'They do. But they also fear us more. . . . The Army functions best when you're afraid of the man above you, and contemptuous of your subordinates.' [14]

Tyranny, fear, hatred – echoes of Hardenburg and Pettinger resound here. And in the continuation of the argument, Cummings' epigrammatic statements sound more and more like gleanings from Dr. Goebbels' notebooks:

'You're misreading history if you see this war as a grand revolution. It's power concentration.'

' . . . politics have no more relation to history than moral codes have to the needs of any particular man.'

'The natural role of twentieth century man is anxiety.'

'The machine techniques of this century demand consolidation, and

---

[13] Mailer, *The Naked and the Dead*, p. 174.
[14] *Ibid.*, pp. 175-76.

with that you've got to have fear, because the majority of men must be subservient to the machine, and it's not a business they instinctively enjoy.' [15]

Hearn is incapable of sustaining a verbal defense against Cummings' remarkably facile attacks. He resorts therefore to a stubborn refusal to admit defeat, and finally, to childish, willful actions, like stubbing out a cigarette on the immaculate floor of the General's tent. It is this incident which leads to the second important ideological exchange between the two men – an exchange which indirectly results in Hearn's death.

Cummings sees the cigarette butt as "a symbol of the independence of his troops, their resistence to him"; sees it as "a threat, a denial of him". But there is no paranoia here as there was in the Executive Officer of the *Atlantis* who demanded to know why the members of the crew hated him; Cumming's reaction is coldly rational. The cigarette butt was a sign that the kind of fear he wanted his subordinates to feel about him, "the unreasoning kind in which his powers were immense and it was effectively a variety of sacrilege to thwart him" was lacking. And "the longer you tarried with resistance the greater it became. It had to be destroyed." [16]

Certain that the culprit was Hearn, Cummings uses dialectics to accuse him of it and at the same time to justify punishment. " 'Have you ever wondered, Robert, why we're fighting this war?' " he asks. And Hearn answers: " 'I don't know. I'm not sure. With all the contradictions, I suppose there's an objective right on our side. That is, in Europe. Over here, as far as I'm concerned, it's an imperialist tossup. Either we louse up Asia or Japan does. And I imagine our methods will be a little less drastic!" But such an off-hand statement does not satisfy the General – nor Mailer. " 'It seems to me, Robert' ", says Cummings, " 'you can do a little better than that' ".

'All right, I can. There's an osmosis in war, call it what you will but the victors always tend to assume the ... the, eh, trappings of the loser. We might easily go Fascist after we win, and then the answer's

15 *Ibid.*, p. 177.
16 *Ibid.*, p. 318.

really a problem.' Hearn puffed at his cigarette. 'I don't go in for the long views. For want of a better idea I just assume it's a bad thing when millions of people are killed because one joker has to get some things out of his system.' [17]

With this speech, Mailer has begun to tie the wars in the two theaters together, has begun to clarify the fight against Fascism in the Pacific. Cummings' lecture-like retort, more than somewhat reminiscent of Hardenburg's lectures to Diestl, clarifies it still further. He proceeds, after a chuckle at Hearn's naivete, to " 'explain the war' " to him:

'I like to call it a process of historical energy. There are countries which have latent powers, latent resources, they are full of potential energy, so to speak. And there are great concepts which can unlock that, express it. As kinetic energy a country is organization, co-ordinated effort, in your epithet, fascism.' He moved his chair slightly. 'Historically, the purpose of this war is to translate America's potential into kinetic energy. The concept of facism, far sounder than communism if you consider it, for it's grounded firmly in men's actual natures, merely started in the wrong country, in a country which did not have enough intrinsic potential power to develop completely. In Germany with that basic frustation of limited physical means there were bound to be excesses. But the dream, the concept was sound enough.' Commings wiped his mouth. 'As you put it, Robert, not too badly, there's a process of osmosis. America is going to absorb that dream, it's in the business of doing it now. When you've created power, materials, armies, they don't wither of their own accord. Our vacuum as a nation is filled with released power, and I can tell you that we're out of the backwaters of history now.'

'We've become destiny, eh?' Hearn said.

'Precisely. The currents that have been released are not going to subside. You shy away from it, but it's equivalent to turning your back on the world. I tell you I've made a study of this. For the past century the entire historical process has been working toward greater and greater consolidation of power. Physical power for this century, an extension of our universe, and a political power, a political organization to make it possible. Your men of power in America, I can tell you, are becoming conscious of their real aims for the first time in our history. Watch. After the war our foreign policy is going to be far more naked, far less hypocritical than it has ever been. We're no

17   *Ibid.*, pp. 319-20.

longer going to cover our eyes with our left hand while our right is extending an imperialist paw.'

Hearn shrugged. 'You think it's going to come about as easily as that? Without resistance?'
'With much less resistance than you think. In college the one axiom you seem to have carried away is that everyone is sick, everyone is corrupt. And it's reasonably true. Only the innocent are healthy, and the innocent man is a vanishing breed. I tell you nearly all of humanity is dead, merely waiting to be disinterred.' [18]

And finally, Cummings narrows the argument down to the particular case at hand:

'I've been trying to impress you, Robert, that the only morality of the future is a power morality, and a man who cannot find his adjustment to it is doomed. There's one thing about power. It can flow only from the top down. When there are little surges of resistance at the middle levels, it merely calls for more power to be directed downward, to burn it out.' [19]

The man who stubbed out the cigarette must be made to admit it, and then must not only be punished, but be made to crawl: " 'The only way you generate the proper attitude of awe and obedience is through immense and disproportionate power.' " [20] Cummings tosses a lighted cigarette at Hearn's feet and orders him to pick it up. After only a momentary hesitation, Hearn obeys; and at this point, his physical, intellectual and moral trial begins.

Abashed by his cowardice, Hearn requests transfer to another section within headquarters and eventually to command of Sgt. Croft's reconnaissance platoom. He feels overwhelmingly the necessity to act, to protest in some manner against fascism as represented by "Generalissimo Cummings". He decides to resign his commission, but before he can put his decision into effect, he is killed in action.

As General Cummings is the indirect cause of Hearn's death, Sgt. Croft is the willing and witting direct cause of it. On the second level of the story, Croft equates with Cummings, as

[18]   *Ibid.*, pp. 321-22.
[19]   *Ibid.*, p. 323.
[20]   *Ibid.*, p. 324.

Dondolo equates with Willoughby. He is non-intellectual, in fact, he is only semi-literate. He is sadistic – witness the scene with the Japanese prisoner cited above. He is a man filled with hate and fear, as is Christian Diestl at the end of *The Young Lions*. But Diestl had at least been capable of human feelings and action; Croft is incapable of them from the outset:

His ancestors pushed and labored and strained, drove their oxen, sweaten their women, and moved a thousand miles. He pushed and labored inside himself and smoldered with an endless hatred.
(You're all a bunch of fuggin whores)
(You're all a bunch of dogs)
(You're all deer to track)
I HATE EVERYTHING WHICH IS NOT IN MYSELF [21]

He represents the physical aspect of Fascism as Cummings represents the intellectual, and on his own level, he desires power as strongly as does Cummings. He alone has commanded the platoon since the invasion and the death of its commanding officer, and he so resents the fact that Hearn has been placed over him that he purposely holds back scouting information about a Japanese machine-gun emplacement and lets Hearn walk directly into point-blank range.

Thus it appears that the Fascists win; Hearn and liberalism are defeated and destroyed. Yet Mailer, interested in warning the reader about the immanent danger of Fascism, not in predicting its eventual pre-eminence, makes this a hollow victory.

General Cummings' strategy for ending the battle of Anopopei includes a pincer attack, frontal and rear, upon the Japanese. To succeed, the plan needs Navy support; to get Navy support, Cummings needs proof that the plan is feasible. He sends the reconnaissance platoon on the scouting expedition on which Hearn is killed, and he leaves for GHQ to argue for the needed destroyers, hoping that a favorable message from the platoon will clinch the argument. But while both Cummings and Croft are away, by a lucky accident, the Japanese General and half his staff are killed and two thirds of the Japanese supplies are either captured or destroyed. American troops penetrate disorganized

[21]   *Ibid.*, p. 164.

enemy lines, and easily roll up the flanks. Before either Cummings or Croft returns, the campaign has concluded. But neither of the apostles of power can claim credit for the victory.

Hearn is dead, unconverted by Cummings, at his death more a liberal than he had ever been before. The destroyer must be ordered back to Headquarters upon its arrival. Croft is unable to complete his mission. The physical victory constitutes an ideological defeat for the two men whom Mailer has implicitly and explicitly labeled Fascistic.

But Mailer does not rest his case on a simple head-on attack on the Fascist villainy represented by Croft and Cummings. Like Myrer, and Burns, and Shaw he feels that unwitting adherence to the Fascist ideology is as dangerous as open commitment to it. Thus, Cummings can call the anti-semitic, anti-Negro and anti-labor views of Lt. Col. Conn a "kind of filth"; nevertheless, he does not reject the views on these grounds – " 'he's more nearly right than you suspect' ", – but on the grounds that such filth is boringly pointless. One sees that Cummings would not hesitate to use the filth pointedly; and that therefore, Conn must be considered an ally of Fascism though he is chauvinistically American and is certainly not politically committed to the Fascist ideology.

In Pvt. Roy Gallagher, Mailer has drawn a protracted portrait of a 100% American as vital as any in the war novels. Gallagher is a stupid, bitter, spiteful man, born and raised in a Studs Lonigan environment in Boston. He sees a fantastic plot by all people who, racially, religiously, or in nationality are different from himself, at the basis of his poverty and inability to get ahead. He joins Christians United, a radically reactionary, semi-military organization whose members are bound together by a mutual hatred of Jews and Communists. He sells a hate magazine on street corners; he electioneers against liberal or labor-supported candidates for public office; he drills with old Springfield rifles at secret meetings once a week. And after war is declared, he attends a special meeting where he hears the following speech:

All right, we're in a war, men, the speaker says, we gotta fight for the country, but we don't want to be forgettin' our private enemies. He pounds the speaker's table over which a flag with a cross is spread. There's the foreign element we got to get rid of, that are conspiring to take over the country. There are cheers from the hundred men seated in camp chairs. We gotta stick together, or we'll be havin' our women raped, and the Red Hammer of Red Jew Fascist Russia WILL BE SMASHING YOUR DOOR DOWN . . .

Who takes away your jobs, who tries to sneak up on your wives and your daughters and even your mothers 'cause they wouldn't stop at nothing, who's out to get YOU and YOU 'cause you aint't a Red and a Jew, and you don't want to bow down before a filthy goddam no-good Communist who don't respect the Lord's name, and would stop at nothing.

Let's kill them! Gallagher shrieks. He is shaking with excitement.

That's it, men, we're gonna clean up on 'em, after the war we're really gonna have an organization, I got telegrams here from our com-*pat*-riots, patriots as well as friends, and they're all stickin' with us. You're all in on the ground floor, men, and those of ya that are goin' into the Army gotta learn to use your weapons so that afterward . . . afterward . . . you get the idea, men. We ain't licked, we're gettin' bigger all the time.[22]

Gallagher is not an ideological fascist, he is not an ideological anything; and this speech is not an ideological appeal. Gallagher is a vicious fool, potentially dangerous, whose danger will remain potential until it is controlled and directed, after the war – perhaps by a General George E. Cummings, who would sneer inwardly at the speech while openly applauding it.

Mailer's points – that Fascism was defeated at least partially by luck; that, because it is a moral not a political evil, its defeat did not preclude its destruction; and that total intellectual as well as emotional commitment are the arms with which it must be fought – are well and convincingly made. The fact that General Cummings' speeches are almost too rational, too argumentatively perfect, to be believable; the fact too that Mailer tends to oversimplify motivation and characterization in terms of sex,[23]

---

[22] *Ibid.*, pp. 277-78.
[23] In sections called "Time Machines", Mailer gives capsulized versions of the pre-war lives of each of his characters. We learn that Gallagher had had a rather unhappy marriage to a somewhat slatternly, dull, boyhood girl friend. We learn that Croft had been a sadistic killer since early youth, that he had killed a man for the thrill of it while on strike-breaking duty with the National Guard, and that his wife had been promiscuously

do not really detract from the novel's conviction. Mailer is certainly one of the most talented writers among the war novelists; in addition to thinking his material through carefully, he presents it with the utmost clarity and precision, and with remarkable skill.

John O. Killens, unfortunately, does not have mailer's talent, his sheer writing ability; few of the war novelists have. His naturalistic-realistic style, like Theodore Dreiser's, is often clumsy, heavy, awkward; he tends to be repetitive, often blurring his point while attempting to clarify it. Still, *And Then We Heard the Thunder* is as convincing and sincere a novel as *The Naked and the Dead,* largely because it has the most socially "given" subject matter of all of the ideological novels which contain American Fascists as their villains: The Negro soldier in the Army of the United States. It is a far more potent subject than one dealing with the Jewish soldier since, despite the admitted anti-semitism of many individual officers and enlisted men, the Jew was treated by and large as a white man co-equal with his fellows. Killens makes this point abundantly clear in his portrayal of Lt. Samuels, a liberal Jew who desires sincerely to be the friend of the Negro troops in his command, who argues that he should be accepted because, as a Jew, he understands their problems, and who is rebuffed simply because he is not a Negro and all the argument and all the sympathy in the world will not make him one.[24] The Jew in the armed services was not asked to behave as a second-class citizen; he was not officially demeaned. One gets the feeling that Irwin Shaw stretches the truth

unfaithful to him. And we learn that Cummings had been cowed by his powerful father, babied into a touch of effiminacy by his doting mother, and, in the inevitable compromise, had developed into a discerning opportunist. But the compromise has resulted in near impotence tinged with homosexuality, and Cummings directs his tremendous energies toward advancing his military career while his wife is forced into infidelity. It should be noted however that Mailer's tendency to oversimplify in this direction prevents his social criticism from becoming oversimple. Thus, his emphasis on sex operates in a manner beneficial as well as detrimental to the artistry of his novel.

[24] The argument is strikingly similar to James Baldwin's in *Another Country* and in many of his essays.

a bit in his portrayal of the persecution of Noah Ackerman, and this takes some of the edge off his anger; but one knows that Negroes were segregated, put into labor battalions, denied most of the rights of free Americans. Killens' anger seems truly justified, for his anti-American-fascism is grounded in reality.

However, despite – or because of – Killens' firm convictions and just anger, he is willing to lean on the givenness of his subject, and unwilling, or unable to plumb the depths of ideological argument. As a consequence, he oversimplifies motivation far more seriously than does Mailer; his Negroes, with the exception of Solly Saunders, the protagonist, remain Negroes; representational, even occasionally symbolic, they never become men. And his white villains are all either anonymous, or if identified, inarticulate "peckerwoods". They are theme-ridden, with neither the desire nor the ability to act or express themselves rationally. To put it another way, if *The Naked and the Dead* is flawed because General Cummings talks too much, *And Then We Heard the Thunder* is equally flawed because Captain Rutherford talks too little. The nature of the characters as victims or villains is built into the novel by its extremely strong subject, and the novel is correspondingly weakened, much as the World War I novels of Humphrey Cobb and Dalton Trumbo were weakened. But, again reminiscent of *Paths of Glory* and *Johnny Got His Gun*, *And Then We Heard the Thunder* paradoxically remains a very powerful book simply because of the strength of its subject.

It is the story of a Negro Company from its formation, through its basic training in Georgia and its heroic action in combat, to a race riot at a rest area in Bainbridge, Australia. The story is told from the point of view of Solly Saunders, an intelligent, ambitious, well-educated northern Negro who goes into the army feeling that the war against Fascism is justified and necessary: " 'If Hitler conquered America, the Negro would be a hundred times worse off than he is now' ",[25] Solly says in answer to an argument that the Negro's real enemy is the Southern white

[25]   John O. Killens, *And Then We Heard the Thunder*, p. 17.

supremacist. " 'This is not a racial war. This is a war of democracy against Fascism pure and simple, and if you're for Tojo, you're for Hitler.' "[26] And he concludes: " 'you might as well let the facts hit you in the face. Hitler and Tojo and the governor of Georgia are on the same damn team. All three of them are against you and me. And it makes no sense to root for one and throw brickbats at the others.' "[27]

He is answered by a character named Scotty that " 'They put me in this cracker army against my will and had the nerve to put me under a peckerwood officer and send me to Georgia. Them Japs and Germans ain't done me nothing. These crackers is my natural enemy.' "[28] Though he never becomes pro-German or pro-Japanese, Solly does become gradually convinced that the true Fascist enemy for the Negro wears the same uniform he does. "The American Army is based on Herrenvolk",[29] he admits to himself at the beginning of the novel, but it takes time and bitter experience for him to become convinced that this is terribly true.

The first experience comes when he is picked up at an Army bus stop by the Ebbensville, Georgia police for being AWOL. Solly argues that they have no jurisdiction, but they take him in anyway. Solly insists that the MPs be called, whereupon an MP Colonel, whose accent betrays him as a northerner, appears. The Colonel rebuffs Solly's pleas calling him "nigger", and Solly attacks him. Subdued and held by two Georgia policemen, Solly is beaten about the thighs and crotch by the Colonel with a nightstick until he loses consciousness.

Because of the beating, Solly and a friend write letters to Negro newspapers protesting racism in the Army. The letters are signed by a number of the men in the Company, all of whom are subsequently transferred, along with other malcontents in the Battalion, to an amphibious combat outfit. Ironically, Captain Rutherford, Solly's original commanding officer, is put in com-

[26]   *Ibid.*, p. 47.
[27]   *Ibid.*, p. 48.
[28]   *Ibid.*, p. 86.
[29]   *Ibid.*, p. 71.

mand of the new Company of "Special Men" as punishment for allowing the malcontents to flourish.

Rutherford, a southerner, is set up as Solly's chief antagonist; in fact, he is the only identifiable ideological villain in the novel. He has cultivated a northern accent, but he lapses into southernisms – "boy" and "nigra" – when excited or angry; because of his general attitude toward command and toward his men, the troops dub the Company "Cap'n Charley's Plantation". Because Solly has the highest I.Q. in the Company, including Rutherford's, the Captain makes him Company clerk; and because Solly is ambitious and believes in the war, Rutherford is able to use him for a time to keep the men in line. One of Solly's tasks is the delivery of Information and Orientation "Why We Fight" lectures; he performs it well until, after many disillusioning experiences with the Army and with war, he simply can no longer believe the things he is supposed to say, and he rebels. Rutherford in a fit of anger breaks him to private.

But Rutherford is not a solid villain, not a worthy antagonist for Solly. His villainy is ignorance and arrogance; he is no Cummings, or Pettinger, or Hardenburg. Certainly, he is "real" enough; there were undoubtedly more Rutherfords than Cummingses in the Army. But he is not very interesting and his usefulness is limited; and so, after he has motivated Solly's rebellion, Killens kills him off, leaving only the white man's Army – impersonal, omnipresent, omnipotent, capricious – as the villain. "Here we are supposed to be fighting against the racist theories of Hitler", Solly thinks, "and we find the same theories holding forth in our own so-called democratic Army. The wonder is that the Negro soldier is not a hundred times more bitter." [30]

He becomes more bitter by the end of the novel. Tension mounts as southern white troops are moved into the Bainbridge rest area, and as all of the nicest restaurants and pubs are gradually put off-limits to Negroes. The Negroes challenge the off limits order and there are clashes with MPs which finally and inevitably result in a full scale battle between whites and Negroes,

[30] *Ibid.*, p. 219.

"the profoundest battle for democracy that any Yankee Army fought on all the far-flung battlefields of World War II",[31] as Solly puts it.

Small arms, machine guns, grenades – all are used; and the fighting lasts until the equipment and the men are finished, dried out. Then Solly walks along the street, among the white and the black dead and wounded, and he thinks:

> They were not bastardly bastards . . . and there were white folks back in the States who were not bastard bastards, they meant well but did so poorly, he wanted desperately to believe goddamit, it was his country as much as it was anybody else's, and he loved it angrily and critically, and he hated the phony patriots, the goddamn goose stepping flag-waving patriots, who really loved the status quo more than they loved the country and its promises unfulfilled.[32]

The goose stepping patriots, the American Fascists – these were the real enemy of the Negro soldier; it was against them, Killens is saying, that World War II was really fought. " 'No peace – ' " Solly says angrily at the novel's close: " 'there is no peace – there is no peace till freedom. You can't make a man a slave and him live in peace with you.' " [33]

Much more evidence could be cited from *And Then We Heard the Thunder* that at least some Negro soldiers recognized and rebelled against the native Fascism inherent in American racist ideas. The villain in the novel *is* the ideas, represented only occasionally by individuals such as Captain Rutherford. In this, Killens diverges somewhat from those other war novelists who individualized their villains as Willoughby and Dondolo, as Cummings and Croft; and he diverges as well from novelists like Myrer and Burns who, though they neither personified villainy in specific characters, still they spread their criticism of America and her institutions over a much broader spectrum than racism. But the differences are relatively unimportant; the second face of villainy is readily identifiable in Killens' book, and his heroes,

[31]   *Ibid.*, p. 438.
[32]   *Ibid.*, p. 465.
[33]   *Ibid.*, p. 484.

Solly and Lt. Samuels, are intellectuals, just as are the heroes of the other novels we have discussed.

Interestingly enough, this was not always true of the ideological novel, as we shall see in the following chapter.

V. TWO DISSENTING VOICES

The preceeding two chapters have been an extended examination of what might justly be called the negative ideological aspects of the war novels. The focus in them has been on fascism, the novelists' definition of it, identification of it, hatred and fear of it. It has been a very one-sided discussion, reflecting the fact that the great majority of the novelists were in remarkable agreement in their beliefs concerning why the war was fought and whom or what it was fought against. We shall see that they agreed substantially on how it had to be fought, by what sort of men with what sorts of ideas and hopes, if it was to be won.

But the agreement in neither case was unanimous. A very important and very vocal minority dissented strongly from the majority's conclusions, and it would be wise, before proceeding to a discussion of the positive aspects of the novels, to attend to their dissenting voice. For the nature of their dissent can help to clarify, by contrast, the negative aspects of the majority's ideological position on the one hand; and on the other, again by contrast, it can prepare the way for a clearer understanding of the positive aspects.

The two writers who spoke loudest and most successfully for the minority were Herman Wouk in *The Caine Mutiny* and James Gould Cozzens in *Guard of Honor*. Like the majority, both of these novelists supported the war; indeed, both favored bending every effort and making every sacrifice to win it. Like the majority too, both were apparently anti-Fascit; however, their anti-Fascism, when it is explicitly stated as in the confrontation scene between Keefer and Greenwald in *The Caine Mutiny*, is clearly limited to the German enemy. These two attitudes – a broad acceptance of the war coupled with a narrow definition of fascism – in combination lead Wouk and Cozzens along a far different ideological path from that followed by the other novelists. When Wouk and Cozzens suggest bending every effort, they mean just that. They feel that a man's duty in a war is to think positively, to close his eyes to ironies, to relinquish his conscience to men and institutions which, bad as they might be, operate expediently for the greatest good of the greatest number. In both novels, the sacrifice of human rights and dignities is demanded for the sake of victory. Both novelists espouse total and absolute commitment to the war effort, but both oppose total commitment to the fight against fascist tendencies wherever and under whatever guise they might appear. Thus, unlike the majority, they refuse to expose and attack Fascist tendencies in America or in her armed services. They not only do not attack the tendencies, but, implicitly admitting they exist, they defend them as expediencies and attack instead those who protest them. And since those who protest are intellectuals by virtue of sufficient sophistication to perceive the ironies, and liberals by virtue of their protest, Wouk and Cozzens are forced to align themselves with the forces of anti-intellectualism and anti-liberalism, and against the majority of the ideological war novelists. They do so willingly. The truly dangerous characters in *The Caine Mutiny* and *Guard of Honor* are intellectual liberals, men who would be heroes to Heym, or Mailer, or Shaw; in fact, Lt. Keefer, the brain behind the *Caine* mutiny, is also a novelist, writing and publishing the sort of novel – apparently a blast against the services – which Heym, Mailer, or Shaw might have written, and which Wouk obviously disapproves of.

Yet, for nearly 450 of its 498 pages, *The Caine Mutiny* itself appears to be a service-blasting, liberal intellectual novel. Lt. Commander Philip F. Queeg, Captain of the *Caine,* a mine sweeper on duty in the Pacific, is a vicious, small-minded career officer with paranoic tendencies. To his sick mind, all actions or incidents which ran counter to his plans or ideas were evidence of a gigantic plot against his authority, and he reacted arbitrarily and capriciously with petty acts of meanness.[1] He frequently cuts off water or coffee for the whole crew as punishment for minor infractions. He suspends movies for six months because someone failed to inform him that a performance was about to start. He develops the habit of summoning his officers at the oddest hours of the day or night, demanding investigations and written reports of the trivia which assumes such tremendous proportions in his own mind: such trivia as a burnt out silex, or a seaman caught with his shirttail hanging out. Often his meanness is not really petty; when a seaman named Stilwell attempts fraudulently, and unsuccessfully, to obtain a Red Cross leave in order to check on rumors of his wife's unfaithfulness, Captain Queeg tries vindictively to retaliate by rigging a summary courts-martial so that Stilwell will receive a Bad Conduct Discharge.

Queeg's attempt to rig the courts-martial – by obtaining Stilwell's confession under duress, and by instructing the under officers of the *Caine* who make up the courts-martial board, in private interviews, to find the seaman guilty – does not work.[2] The board flies in the face of Queeg's bitter anger and threats, to mete out only token punishment. Queeg's threats bear fruit only in sulking pettiness, but Lt. Keefer sees much meaning in the Captain's attitudes and actions in the Stilwell case, and he uses his conclusions to convince the other officers, especially Lt. Maryk, the *Caine's* executive officer, that there is latent danger in Queeg's obvious mental problems. Articulate, self-confident, Keefer gives Maryk a slick psychoanalysis of the Captain:

'... He hates Stilwell for being handsome, healthy, young competent, and naturally popular and attractive – all the things that Queeg is not. Ever read *Billy Budd*, by Melville? Read it. That's the whole story.

---

[1] Note the similarity between Queeg and the Executive Officer of the *Atlantis* in *The Deep Six*, though Queeg's paranoia is hardly suicidal. Note also the similarity between Queeg and Captain Morton in Thomas Heggan's *Mr. Roberts*. Despite the humor in the situations involving Morton, there are serious overtones to Heggan's characterization of him. He has no really redeeming features; no heart of gold beneath his gruff exterior. He is being laughed at, not with, and he is therefore a close counterpart of Queeg.

[2] Herman Wouk, *The Caine Mutiny*, pp. 258-70.

Stilwell is a symbol of all the captain's frustrations, all the things he would like to smash because he can't have them, like a child wanting to break another child's toys. Infantilism is very strong in our captain. I'm leaving out a conjectural element which I also think is important, maybe even decisive – the sexual –' Maryk made a disgusted grimace. ' – I know, we start wading in slime at this point. But repressed desire can turn to hate, and all of the captain's maladies could fall into a pattern on the theory of an unconscious, violently repressed inversion. . . . ' [3]

Lt. Maryk, sincere, methodical, slow-witted, knows that the Captain resents Stilwell because the seaman had committed a blunder for which Queeg was blamed. He deflates Keefer's neat analysis of homosexualism, but he suspects that Keefer is correct in his assumption that Queeg is dangerously neurotic. But he feels that the charge demands more evidence, and to this end, he begins to keep a secret log of Queeg's actions subsequent to the courts-martial. In the log, besides reporting all of the relatively minor abuses of authority cited above, Maryk records two instances of apparent cowardice on Queeg's part.

The first of these occurs while the *Caine* acts as a landing craft escort at the invasion of Kwajalein Atoll. Under Queeg's command, the ship outspeeds the escorted vessels to the departure point, drops a yellow dye marker as a guide for the vessels, and proceeds at full speed away from possible shore battery fire.[4] The second instance occurs at the invasion of Saipan: a destroyer 1000 yards on the *Caine's* beam is hit by shore batteries, and, though the Caine's guns are on target and ready to fire, Queeg orders the ship to pull away from the impending battle at twenty knots.[5]

Reluctantly, with some prodding from Keefer, Maryk comes to admit that the captain may be a dangerous paranoic. The evidence in the log is undeniable: the most damning entry is a pathetically comic incident in which all of the officers are forced to search the ship from top to bottom, and to search the enlisted men's clothing as they stand naked before them, trying to find

[3] *Ibid.*, p. 268.
[4] *Ibid.*, pp. 237-39.
[5] *Ibid.*, pp. 272-74.

a key which an unknown seaman had apparently used to pilfer the wardroom stores of a quart of strawberries.[6]

Maryk resolves to report Queeg as unfit to command by reason of illness under Article 184 of Navy Regulations. Aware of his own shortcomings in an argument, and of Keefer's articulateness, Maryk tries to convince Keefer to go with him to make the report, using the log as evidence. At the crucial moment however, Keefer, the intellectual liberal catalyst of Maryk's log, loses his nerve. He points out that while the log would convince any psychiatrist, it could not possibly convince an admiral. Furthermore, the Navy system protects Queeg, he says, not Queeg's crew from Queeg. Angrily shaken by Keefer's cowardice, the honest Maryk postpones his action.[7]

But Article 184 provides not only for the relief by Navy Department order of a commanding officer unfit, for physical, ethical, or moral reasons to command, but "When reference to such higher authority is undoubtedly impracticable", it also provides for his immediate relief by a subordinate without such an order. And when the Caine is caught in a typhoon, and Queeg's orders become contradictory; when Maryk becomes firmly convinced that Queeg's continued command will endanger the ship and its crew, Maryk finally takes over, bringing the Caine safely through the typhoon, and leaves himself open to the charge of mutiny.[8]

His defense of course is based upon Article 184, and after a long and bitter trial in which Maryk's log is Exhibit A for the defense, and Queeg unwittingly its chief witness, skilfully led to betray his megalomania and his paranoia in cross examination by Lt. Greenwald, the defense attorney – as adept an amateur psychoanalist as Keefer – Maryk's action is partially vindicated, and the charge of mutiny is dismissed.[9]

To this point, The Caine Mutiny is similar to the other ideo-

---

[6] Ibid., pp. 287-99.
[7] Ibid., pp. 311-16.
[8] Ibid., pp. 328-45.
[9] Ibid., pp. 348-440. The Caine Mutiny Court-Martial became a quite successful Broadway play and movie, following faithfully section VI of the novel, "The Court-Martial", pp. 348-448.

logical war novels, despite Keefer's dishonest irresolution. Queeg, at best a dangerous psychopath and at worst an incipient Fascist, has been stripped of his command. The forces of justice and right, of freedom, appear to have triumphed. But at the denouement, dominated by Lt. Greenwald, one of the most drastic and inexplicable shifts in intention among all of the war novels takes place. Half drunk, Greenwald attends the party celebrating Maryk's acquittal – and incidentally, celebrating the acceptance of Keefer's war novel for publication – and declares that the trial was a miscarriage of justice, that Maryk is guilty, and that Queeg actually is a hero. Greenwald is Jewish, and he argues that the only thing that kept the Nazis from invading America and melting his mother down for soap were " 'these birds we call regulars – these stuffy, stupid Prussians in the Navy and the Army' ".[10] " 'Yes, even Queeg, poor sad guy, yes, and most of them not sad at all, fellows, a lot of them sharper boys than any of us, don't kid yourself, best men I've ever seen, you can't be good in the Army or Navy unless you're goddamn good. Though maybe not up on Proust 'n' *Finnegan's Wake* and all.' " [11]

Queeg is not a dangerous paranoic and a coward, all of the evidence of 400 pages to the contrary; and Maryk had no right to usurp Queeg's authority under Article 184 or any others – the action was really mutinous. But Maryk is only partially responsible for thinking Queeg ill, and is consequently only half guilty of the mutiny. Greenwald turns on Keefer, the reader of Proust and Joyce and *Billy Budd,* the writer of novels, and suddenly unmasks him as the true villain of the piece:

'I defended Steve [Maryk] because I found out the wrong guy was on trial. Only way I could defend him was to sink Queeg for you. I'm sore that I was pushed into the spot, and ashamed of what I did, and thass why I'm drunk. Queeg deserved better at my hands. I owed him a favor, don't you see? He stopped Hermann Goering from washing his fat behind with my mother.' [12]

And with this, Greenwald sloshes champagne into Keefer's face.

Formally and ideologically, *The Caine Mutiny* collapses here,

[10] *Ibid.,* p. 446.
[11] *Ibid.,* p. 447.
[12] *Ibid.,* p. 448.

at the denouement, at the point where it should peak. Wouk apparently changed his mind about what he wanted the book to say by the time he was ready to finish it, thus he attempts to whitewash one of the most believable villains in all World War II literature in this fantastic, unprepared for, grossly sentimentalized scene.[13]

Guard of Honor does not suffer the same collapse for it never pretends to be what it is not. It is a straightforward defense of the status quo, a clear, unmistakable attack on intellectual liberalism, and a strong argument for middle-of-the-road white supremacy. As does Wouk, Cozzens makes heroes of those who would be villains in the majority of the ideological novels, especially in such a novel as *And Then We Heard the Thunder,* and villains of those who would be heroes. But he does not hide his position, nor resort to such devices as a surprise ending in order to present it. The principal plot line in *Guard of Honor* concerns the proposed training of an all-Negro medium bomber group at Ocanara, a Florida air base. The Negroes of course are denied the freedom of the Florida city near the base, but, largely to placate the delicate sensibilities of the civilian population, they are also segregated on the base, given separate but equal living, mess, and Officer's Club facilities. A good deal of the book is given over to a discussion of the integration-segregation issue in the services. Cozzens' position is clear. At best he feels that, if integration will upset the delicate balance between servicemen at an American base and the civilians surrounding the base, and thus hamper the war effort, it must be sacrificed; at worst, Cozzens is an articulate exponent of segregationism, arguing for a cautious, careful, gradual integration on the South's own terms.

Lt. Edsell, a liberal-intellectual writer in the Public Relations

---

[13] William H. Whyte, Jr. devotes Chapter 19 of *The Organization Man* pp. 269-75, to a discussion of *The Caine Mutiny.* Whyte's conclusions and mine are quite similar, though he sees in Wouk's message a manifestation of the modern American's tendency toward conformity only, and does not connect this with Fascism as I have tried to do. Whyte is a bit careless with his evidence, unfortunately, calling Keefer an ex-writer, and asserting that Greenwald's mother had been killed in Germany ("boiled down for soap") whereas it was really an aunt and uncle in Cracow.

Office at the base, is an equivalent of Lt. Keefer. He is potentially as dangerous to the status quo as Keefer, though not nearly so successful in his attempts to upset it. Edsell is a loud-mouthed, Northern trouble-maker who argues nastily against segregation with anyone who will listen to or challenge him. But, unlike Keefer, largely because of his intolerant integrationism and because of his brashness, Edsell convinces no one and antagonizes everyone, even fellow Northerners who might be expected to sympathize with his views. Capt. Nathaniel Hicks, Special Projects PRO visiting the base to do a magazine story which is to include the training of the Negro pilots, asks Edsell: " 'For God's sake, Jim, do you have to argue all the time? Can't you just think what you think, keep still, and let us work?' " [14] And WAC Lt. Amanda Turck – who, along with Hicks, supplies the love interest in the novel – after being told by Edsell that " 'something might be made out of you. You have a nasty disposition, which is the first thing you need if you're going to stand up to those sons of bitches. . . . Don't tell me you like swallowing their crap! I don't think you want to see people walked on either!' " replies " 'Oh no! . . . No, you don't. I don't have to join up with you – or else! This is a free country, my fine big-hearted liberal friend!' " [15]

But Cozzens allows the utter deflation of Edsell to be accomplished by Capt. Wiley, a gentleman, a fighter pilot, and a Southerner, Edsell argues for a form of mutiny by the Negro flyers, argues that they ought to get themselves arrested by trying to force their way into the Officers' Club:

'They have a chance to force the issue, and maybe end this whole segregation business, once and for all. The Army can't afford to practice segregation, if it's known they do. They'd have to allow Negroes the same rights as white men; and once that was established, I don't think the rights could later be taken away, even in the South – '

'They don't rate the same rights as white men', Captain Wiley said gently [Edsell simply speaks, but clearly without gentleness; he is given to "thoughtfully picking his nose" when he does speak gently]. 'That's

<hr />

[14] James Gould Cozzens, *Guard of Honor*, p. 337 .
[15] *Ibid.*, p. 305.

why the same rights aren't and can't be allowed them. The worst thing that could happen to them would be to end segregation. That would mean that a white man in the South would have to act every day as an individual to protect himself. That would be very bad for the Negroes. With segregation, now, both parties know where they stand, so there's almost no friction, see? Except when somebody from outside comes in and stirs it up. Your idea is mighty dangerous, Lieutenant.'

Wiley's is the really dangerous idea, Edsell asserts: " 'It is very dangerous to deny people their rights. It means that, in the long run, you drive them to take their rights by force.' " Wiley replies:

'That, friend, they never will do, because they can't. . . . What you're trying to say is that a Negro is equal to a white man. Don't you see that if he was equal, you wouldn't have to be demanding "rights" for him? Like you say, he'd have them by force, if no other way. He hasn't got them, though they gave them to him, and more, after the War Between the States. But he couldn't keep them; he wasn't up to it. That's where the North was wrong then, and that's where you're wrong now. The two races just aren't equal. Anyone who says they are, either doesn't have good sense, or doesn't know Negroes. . . .

'No amount of changes, and nothing I could do, would change the fact that a Negro happens to be a member of a relatively inferior race; physically, mentally, every way. It may be too bad, from his standpoint, and yours; but it's true.'

Edsell calls this an unscientific statement which no anthropologist could or would accept, " 'Outside some of Hitler's phoneys' "; to which Wiley replies, "Please don't call me a liar, Lieutenant.' " Edsell rapidly backs and fills:

'Who called you a liar?. . . . A liar is a person who says what he knows isn't true; but it never occurred to me that you would know it wasn't true and still be saying it. That leaves you out, as far as I'm concerned. However, if you mean I'm not free to say that a statement which I know to be untrue it a lie, get rid of the notion. Captain. I believe you can't help your prejudices. I think if you could, you surely would; because nobody likes to make himself absurd. I wish I could help you straighten out your thinking; but it doesn't look as if I could, and I've got to get downtown; so we may as well drop it.'

'I believe that would be a right smart thing for us to do,' Captain Wiley said. 'I appreciate your wanting to help me, Lieutenant; and I'm glad that you did not call me a liar.' [16]

[16] *Ibid.*, pp. 336, 337, 338, and 339.

Cozzens' attitude toward Edsell, and consequently, toward liberalism, intellectualism, and racial equality is abundantly clear here. He even reinforces it by making Edsell a non-combat desk soldier while Wiley holds the Distinguished Flying Cross for his services to the RAF before the United States entered the war.[17] Clearly, from Cozzens' point of view, Wiley and Wiley's ideas merit the reader's sympathy far more than Edsell and his ideas. In any of the other ideological novels, except possibly *The Caine Mutiny,* their positions would have been reversed.

Though Lt. Edsell equates with Lt. Keefer from *The Caine Mutiny,* there is in *Guard of Honor* no narrow-minded, stupid bully with paranoic Fascist tendencies who might equate with Captain Queeg. Nor has Cozzens resorted to a sentimentalized, flag-waving caricature of the courageously suffering Jew for his ideological spokesman. Instead of Queeg or Lt. Greenwald, Cozzens speaks through Col. Norman Ross, a character far more convincing than either of Wouk's people, or than both of them in combination.

Ross, a judge in civilian life, and called Judge throughout the novel, is the older and wiser head who actually operates the Ocanara air base for the boyish flying hero Major General "Bus" (for "Buster") Beal. Ross opposes the original segregation order, issued impetuously by a foolish colonel named Mowbray, on the grounds that it might result in bad public relations, and might even draw a reprimand from the Pentagon. No principles are involved; Ross is concerned purely with the practical, expedient aspects of the situation. The Pentagon does react. It orders that the potential trouble on the base be somehow averted, and Ross assumes the task of averting it. He handles the situation very

---

[17] The fact that Lt. Edsell is not a combat soldier is emphasized heavily by Cozzens. Lt. Col. Carricker, who is court-martialed and acquitted for striking one of the Negro pilots after an error in judgment by the Negro had almost resulted in a serious air tragedy (pp. 87-88), is the holder of the Distinguished Service Cross with oak leaf cluster; and Capt. Wiley, as we have seen, had been decorated by the RAF before the United States entered the war. Edsell, for all his big talk, is portrayed as a coward – and a coward of the worst sort, the sort that runs from combat (as he does when he backs down to Wiley) not the sort that collapses under combat pressures.

cleverly, explaining to the Negro pilots that racial considerations have nothing to do with placing such buildings as the Officers' Club off limits: " 'This is the Army. There are no Army Regulations that make any distinction on the basis of race, creed, or color.' " The buildings have been placed off limits because, " 'The use of them, along with permanent party personnel having no connection with your group, would work against the development of that group spirit which it is one of the most important objects of this project to inculcate.' " [18]

This is the sort of speech an institution like the Army wants; Ross is perfectly equipped, psychologically, morally, and ethically to deliver it. He holds to no principles, outside of loyalty to the status quo represented by his superiors in the Army hierarchy from the Pentagon on down to Gen. Beal. Principles are nonsense, believed in only by the grossly ignorant: "Though the level of intelligence in the average man might be justly considered low, in very few of them would it be so low that they accepted notions that they fought, an embattled band of brothers, for noble 'principles'." [19] He holds to the idea of expediency in justification of all his thought and actions, and he searches confidently for an explanation in these terms of the thought and actions of others. When his wife protests that the Negro officers have a point, he answers:

'Whether you like it or not, there are things you can't buck – no matter how much you want to, how vital it is to you. . . . For reasons of justice and decency; and also for reasons of political policy, the War Department decided that colored men must be given the chance to quality as officers. We have about a thousand of them in the Air Force, we have now somewhere around three hundred thousand white officers. A certain number of these, I don't know how many, but in relation to the whole, a proportion infinitely larger than that of colored to white officers, hold that a nigger is a nigger. They will not have anything to do with him socially. That is their decision, inculcated in them from their first conscious moments, handed down to them with the sanctions of use and interest. I don't say that this couldn't be changed, or that it won't ever be; but it won't change

18   *Ibid.*, p. 238.
19   *Ibid.*, p. 275.

today, tomorrow, next week: A man cannot choose to see what he cannot see.[20]

Furthermore, a man does not always truly see what he thinks he sees. Ross' wife argues that since the majority is for Negro rights, then they should prevail. The colonel answers:

'That a big majority may feel that a Negro is a human being all right; but when you add that they want to see him treated fairly, you're wrong. That is not the condition. The condition is that the big majority doesn't *mind* if he's treated fairly, a very different thing. The big majority does not want him to marry their sister. The big majority does not want to insult or oppress him; but the big majority has, in general, a poor opinion of him.' [21]

Like it or not, agree or not, this is about as clear and objective an appraisal of white attitudes toward the Negro as can be found in any novel. Cozzens, through Ross, puts his finger squarely on that which complicates beyond all possibility of easy solution the problem of equal civil rights for the Negro: the tendency of those who wish him well to "tolerate" him. But Ross is not always objective, and when he ventures an opinion – when he states his own, and Cozzens' attitude – it comes out white supremacy:

Behind the black face might be a courageous spirit and a sharp intelligence; but you must expect both to be damped and spoiled by the inbred resignation, the experience of generations bitterly resenting, yet always resenting impotently, the white man's yoke. Every day the white man's greed and folly proved that his claimed superiority was a lie. He was not clever; he was not strong; he was not good; he was nobody's born master. All he was, was, to a black man's sorrow and his shame, a little too much for most black men.[22]

Ross gives legal and philosophical substance and weight to the arguments of Wiley, though neither man knows the other. We have here a Croft-Cummings or Dondolo-Willoughby kind of alliance with the very important difference that, while Mailer and Heym made these alliances villainous, Cozzens treats Ross and Wiley as heroes. White supremacy, segregation, the authori-

---

tarianism of the armed services – these are the sorts of things the majority of the ideological novelists fought against. Cozzens clearly defends them; Ross sees to it that the segregation order stands and the Negro officers who challenge it are gently reprimanded and firmly returned to their 'place'. "All discord, harmony not understood"; he quotes mentally: "All partial evil, universal good." [23] The chain of command and the chain of being equate; this best of all possible worlds is to be defended, not changed. Wartime is a time for doing one's job, coolly, rationally; loyally; it is certainly not a time to fight for social reform. The solution to the problem of evil according to Wouk and Cozzens is the denial of evil's existence; or better, the rationalization of its existence in terms of the struggle against a 'greater' evil. *The Caine Mutiny* says this clearly and potently; *Guard of Honor* seconds it, not quite so specifically, but certainly as potently.

Both Wouk and Cozzens write extremely well, and for this reason alone it might be argued that they perform a service for the American literature of the war. Despite Wouk's inexplicable shift in intention, despite his insistence on opening and closing his story through the point of view of a relatively minor character, Willie Keith, as if it were some sort of *bildungsroman*; and although Cozzens' intricate and highly sophisticated style, replete with flashbacks and simultaneous points of view, is often more puzzling than enlightening – these are two of the best made novels to come out of the war. Indeed, Malcolm Cowley, in a review of Cozzens' *By Love Possessed,* called *Guard of Honor* "still [nine years after its publication] the most thoughtful, the most brilliantly organized and the best written of all the American novels of the World War II".[24]

It might be argued too, as Cowley argues with the phrase "most thoughtful", that Wouk and Cozzens perform yet a greater service for the war novel by portraying the opposite, less widely disseminated and less popular side of the ideological coin. They

[23] *Ibid.*, p. 535.
[24] Malcolm Cowley, New York Times Book Review, LXII (August 25, 1957), 1.

do not find a fascist behind every bar or leaf or star. They deny that there is anything inherently or necessarily good in either intellectualism or liberalism; a man can be both of these and still be a loud-mouth, a coward, and a phony like Edsell and Keefer. They assert that one can be paranoic, conservative, and even a middle-of-the-road white supremacist without being a committed Fascist.

But it is clear that in the process of performing this latter service, Wouk and Cozzens reject an all-out involvement in the physical-moral-ideological struggle against Fascism. It is clear that they affirm authoritarianism, conservatism, and anti-intellectualism, that they support nearly all of the ideas and attitudes opposed by the majority of the war novelists, and oppose those supported by them. It might be argued that their approach, their arguments, their conclusions amount really to a counter-ideology; it might be argued, as the majority of the novelists, upon the evidence of their own works, would probably argue, that Wouk and Cozzens are in reality little more than ideological neo-Fascists.

And with this probable judgment in mind – whether it be right or wrong, just or unjust – we are now prepared to examine closely the positive ideological aspects of the majority of the war novels.

VI. THE TWO FACES OF COMMITMENT

The American soldier's war aim, James Gould Cozzens opines through Col. Ross

was to get out as soon as possible and go home. This didn't mean that he wouldn't fight – on the contrary. Brought within fighting distance of the enemy, he saw well enough that until those people over there were all killed or frightened into quitting, he would never get home. He did not need to know about their bad acts and wicked principles. Compared to the offense they now committed by being here, and by shooting at him and so keeping him here, any alleged atrocities of theirs, and evil schemes of their commanders, were trifles.[1]

And Arthur Miller in *Situation Normal,* a non-fiction account of his travels to army camps in pursuit of facts and atmosphere to aid him in writing the screenplay of Ernie Pyle's "Story of G. I. Joe", speaks of resenting "the wide-spread, wise-guy notion that Belief is unnecessary because we have no men in the army who are affected either way by such factors".[2] Although he is troubled because "never in any of these calculations about the soldier can I honestly bring in the socio-political context of this war. I can't seem to find men who betray a social responsibility for doing or not doing anything",[3] still he cannot agree with "the wise guy writers" for whom "war is not supposed to make any sense. Soldiers are supposed to be suckers." [4] Neither can he agree with those who think of the soldier as "a kind of mentally helpless puppy, a literal dogface stoically suffering the buffetings of a fate he does not understand, a kind of good schlemiel des-

---

[1] Cozzens, *Guard of Honor,* p. 275.
[2] Arthur Miller, *Situation Normal,* p. 113.
[3] *Ibid.,* p. 44.
[4] *Ibid.,* p. 176.

tined throughout history to take the rap and still give away his candy rations to kids in some newly captured foreign town".[5]

For Miller, the American serviceman is a thinking human being, perhaps reluctant to discuss ideas, but "longing to understand the why of this war and the why of the peace".[6] The soldier's tendency to overlook the spiritual and the idealistic in favor of the physical and animalistic ("Some people say he has no ideas which cannot be summed up in three words; beer, women, and going home"),[7] his refusal to express or discuss ideas, should not be interpreted to mean that he lacks ideas:

... always you sense how afraid they are of being mocked for passing moral judgments. It almost seems that they feel the Fascist merely went out to take what they wanted from the world, to change some fences, and that we had to stop them because one of the fences happened to adjoin our property. It almost sounds like a property owners' war, with either side acting like the other if their real estate holdings were reversed. And yet you know, listening to the way they speak, that they do not want it to be merely a property owners' war because it is a mockery to die for property alone.[8]

Interestingly enough, both writers are correct – to a degree and with qualifications. From 1942 through July, 1945 the Research Branch of the Information and Education Division of the United States War Department collected data relevant to the attitudes of United States servicemen toward the war, the peace, and their own service. The data was edited under the auspices of a Special Committee of the Social Research Council, and was published in four volumes with the title *Studies in Social Psychology in World War II*. The study has all of the weaknesses as well as the strengths of scientific 'objectivity': the editors did not even meet the sample subjects, let alone collect the data themselves, so there was no way for them to be misled by unscientific feelings or impressions; but just because of this, they never really get at the reasons behind the answers to the questions they work with. As a case in point: the editors emphasize over and over again

5   *Ibid.*, p. 6.
6   *Ibid.*, p. 176.
7   *Ibid.*, p. 6.
8   *Ibid.*,pp. 176-77.

that soldiers mistrusted the Army's motivation each time it appeared to be acting altruistically or for the good of the men, and they reacted and adjusted accordingly; yet the editors appear to have overlooked the possibility that, since the data-gathering and -processing was done by the Army, the data itself might not be absolutely trustworthy. Still, the editors are scrupulously honest in identifying whatever deficiencies they discovered in the data, and whatever difficulties they encountered in working with it. And they arrived at some interesting conclusions bearing upon the statements cited above and upon the subject of this chapter as a whole.

On the basis of an agree-disagree-undecided type of questionnaire, plus an optional essay concerned with American war aims, the editors determined that the majority of soldiers either admittedly did not know what they were fighting for or against, or their beliefs were so contradictory as to be worthless. But they also found that the majority believed that they fought to survive, not simply to get home again; and, clearly, that they did not believe that they fought in a property owners' war. The data also showed that a distinct minority (about 15% of the whole, or one-third of those who wrote the optional essay) were ideologically committed to the war, and were capable of verbalizing their commitment. Most of this minority was made up of "better educated men" who "consistently made more favorable response than the less educated on items reflecting personal commitment".[9] But their commitment, ideological though it might be, was not especially idealistic; they were more willing than the less educated for example to express doubts concerning the worth of fighting the war. Neither were they as openly cynical as some of the others; in most cases they felt that winning the war was essential to survival, and that therefore it must be fought through to unconditional surrender. The report continues in an unusually speculative tone:

---

[9] *Studies in Social Psychology in World War Two*, Vol. I, p. 457. See especially Chap. 9 of Vol. I, "The Orientation of Soldiers Toward the War", pp. 430-85 for details which led the editors to the conclusions summarized here.

Perhaps the better educated man's greater acceptance of the idea that they personally would have to see the war through reflected their greater willingness to accept logical consequences or at least their lesser ability to avoid facing unpleasant facts. That is, everyone defined the war as a necessity and everybody agreed that a great many men were needed in the Army. The educated man, however, was likely, somewhat more often than his less educated fellow soldier, to draw from these two premises the conclusion that he personally was needed and to reconcile himself to the results of his logical reasoning.[10]

Thus the study supports both the pessimism of Cozzens and the optimism of Miller, and at the same time challenges both. The great majority of soldiers certainly wanted to go home, but this was not a single, simple desire translated directly into motivation for fighting; and the majority certainly had ideas or notions concerning "the why of this war and the why of the peace", but the ideas were largely garbled and inconsistent, and there is little evidence that they 'longed' for clarification and understanding.

But the minority is most important for our immediate purposes, for the ideological novelists were obviously part of it. In their attitude toward the war and the peace, they quite accurately fit the speculative description of the educated soldier cited above. Indeed, with the exception of Wouk and Cozzens, they go beyond it. For them, the uncommitted majority is a danger sign, a sign which points to the loss of the peace even though the war be won. The victory of Stefan Heym's crusaders is mitigated by the fact that Dondolo and Willoughby return to a lucrative peacetime world; and Mailer's Lt. Hearn, shortly before his death, thinks: "History was in the grasp of the Right, and after the war their big political campaigns would be intense. One big push, one big offensive, and history was theirs for this century, perhaps the next one. The League of Omnipotent Men." [11] The Wouk and Cozzens approach which argues abandonment of principle and makes an expedient virtue of viciousness supplies, the other novelists feel, a perfect climate for the growth of the League, and makes fertile the ideological seedbed nourishing the Cummingses and the Willoughbys.

[10] *Ibid.*, p. 458.
[11] Mailer, *The Naked and the Dead*, p. 391.

But the novelists are not merely Cassandras or Jeremiahs, they suggest positive constructive action to prevent the formation of the League, or to combat it once it has been formed. Their suggestions are not presented as propaganda, or as data to be programmed and percentaged, nonetheless, they are obvious enough to be abstracted from the work and summarized here, as a preface to the discussion of the two faces of commitment which follows.

First of all, the novelists insist, one must be able to recognize the danger; one must be able to generalize from the physical to the ideological, so that the war stands as it were metaphorically or symbolically for the conflict in thought and idea which precipitated it. Thus, one may see Fascism as the exclusive property of no nation or race, may see it not simply as the primary cause of war, but more importantly, as the inevitable result of the very anti-intellectualism, indifference, and complacency advocated by Wouk and Cozzens.

Beyond this, one must see that only through caring, through a sense of personal individual responsibility for the actions and fate of his fellow-man – a sense of responsibility totally incompatible with indifference or complacency – through a feeling even of culpability if one has been cold to the justice of the cause for which the great crusade was being pursued, can the cause prevail.

And so seeing, one may then in complete rational and emotional awareness *voluntarily* involve himself in and commit himself to the cause. Notice the use of the singular here; notice the stress on the word "voluntarily". Enforced commitment is negation. Morality cannot be legislated; hypocrisy may not result in physical defeat, but it can prevent ideological and moral victory. Each individual must not only act – he must *choose* to act.

This deceptively simple schema is complicated for the novelists by a set of paradoxes which have made their presences felt frequently throughout the preceding chapters of this discussion: War is evil, but this war, because it is necessary, is good; this war is necessary in order to defeat Fascism which is consummately evil primarily because it is pragmatically based on the belief that the necessary is the good; the war can only be waged successfully by responsible individuals, but only through the medium of the armed services which by their very nature militate against individualism. Finally, the novelists see the services to be themselves basically Fascistic, which results in the ultimate paradox – evil must be used in behalf of good even though its use insures the continuance of evil.

Wouk and Cozzens either gloss over the paradoxes, as Col. Ross does, on the grounds that the ordinary soldier is not aware of or interested in them anyway, or openly apologize for and defend them in expedient terms, as Lt. Greenwald does. The other novelists are angered by them, and pained, and when they choose commitment despite them, it is with this realization and resolution: that at the root of the paradoxes rests the same expediency and irresponsibility as at the root of Fascism, that the war must be pursued against the root itself, and that only the responsible, committed individual can successfully wage the war. Only such a man, they are convinced, voluntarily eschewing his individualism to act in concert with others, can hope to defeat a Diestle or a Pettinger or to overcome the power of Cummings, Willoughby, and the rest of the League of Omnipotent Men.

The novelists believed that some men knew all of this almost intuitively, while others discovered it or learned it as the war progressed,[12] and these are the two faces of commitment which they portray. The emphasis is on the second face, upon the process of discovery; the first functions as a dialectic antagonist to the noncommitment of the first, or as a conscience, or perhaps, ultimately, as a sacrificial catalyst speeding up the process.

Mad Thorpe in *The Crusaders,* like a Fury circling Yates and jabbing at him with his knowledge of the depth and breadth of the corruption of Willoughby and Dondolo and Loomis, is such a face. So too is Bing, the sensitive German-Jew-American who argues justice and morality with Yates, who, out of the purest of convictions writes the pure corn of the Fourth of July leaflet, and who trips over his own humanity when he lets himself be

[12] Conversely, *Studies in Social Psychology* shows that commitment was highest during the early months of service, and that it decreased gradually as the war progressed.

seduced by a German woman he had known as a boy, and falls into a pit of depression. Both are sacrificed, Bing literally and Thorpe into schizophrenia, in order that Yates may learn that "you couldn't let things ride you; you had to be in the saddle",[13] and that in war "help is an obligation as holy as that of the medic who pulls you, wounded, out of the line";[14] and in order that he may finally use this knowledge against the evils which he finally admits surround him. Noah Ackerman in *The Young Lions,* like Bing, a Jew, functions as the sacrificial victim which galvanizes Michael Whitacre's new-born commitment into action which results in the death of Christian Diestl.

Many of the faces are not so fully drawn as these, or are glimpsed only fleetingly. As suggested in the Introduction, Lt. Lynch in John Hersey's *The War Lover* is such a face, helping to convert Boman from cynicism ("We were up to our tally-whackers in illusions, slogans, shibboleths, belief in magic – mostly out of ads. We were ready to die to the last man for Dinah Shore, rare sirloin, a cold beer, and a Caribean cruise.") to a modified commitment.[15] Lt. Potnik in William Fridley's *A Time to go Home* carries a wounded comrade to safety in the house of some Belgian partisans, wondering seriously for the first time what the war is all about and why he is fighting in it. As if in answer, a short time later one of the partisans says:

'We are still afraid, my son, because we do not know what you will do when the time of peace arrives. Will you continue the parable of the children and remain both generous and cruel? Will you, with the truce, wish to return to your cars and your pictures and your ice cream? Will you desert us when most we need you?

'For you must understand that this war in which you are engaged is a holy war, and though you have beat down the devil, he was alive and fouled the air and his spoor is everywhere. It is then, my son, that the true war begins. It is then that you must climb, naked and shivering, from your steel shelter and grapple in the mud with the powerful spirit of evil.' [16]

And Potnik decides that the time to go home is only when the

13   Heym, *The Crusaders,* p. 175.
14   *Ibid.,* p. 491.
15   Hersey, *The War Lover,* p. 225.
16   William Fridley, *A Time to Go Home,* p. 160.

job is done, and that may be never, but this realization must make no difference. He returns to action, thinking: "among the good ones, among the men of good will, the strong survive and the weak fall by the way. And of the men of good will, the strongest shall have the greatest duty." [17] And the face of Jimmy, the Quiet Man, lying dead after the race riot in *And Then We Heard the Thunder* prompts Solly Saunders to swear "to never forget the way I feel this Monday morning. I will always hate war with all my heart and my soul. I will always fight the men who beat the drums for war in the name of Holy Patriotism in any Nation, any language." [18] In the very ambivalence of Solly's hatred of war and determination to fight resides the commitment that transcends paradox.

But the first face, while it always subserves the conversion of the second, is not always essential to that conversion. Often the discovery and acceptance of commitment emerges from deep within the individual without the example or leadership or sacrifice of one already initiated. Carl Jonas in *Beachhead on the Wind* portrays a sailor who had hidden in his foxhole on the beach from the tremendous struggle with the elements with which the book is largely concerned. As the sailor lay there, "It had come to him sharply that he was the whole war, that on what he did about it, whatever it was, depended the future not just of this operation but that of the campaign, of the country, of the world and the people in it. He was shaking there where he lay in his sack, not with cold but with guilt and with fear." And he rises and goes back, and this act becomes for him "a marvelous burning iridescent thing".[19] And Leggett in *End of a War* becomes his own sacrificial victim in order that he may learn the same things, though clearly, his knowledge lacks the romantic glow. As we have seen, most of the novel is concerned with his struggle to justify the war and his own part in it on individual terms, and in the process he loses touch with reality as his conscience advances to destroy his indifference. At the end of the

[17]   *Ibid.*, p. 224.
[18]   Killens, *And Then We Heard the Thunder*, p. 482.
[19]   Carl Jonas, *Beachhead on the Wind*, p. 204.

novel, he is slowly finding a new self, rising out of his self-inflicted purgatory:

Leggett pulled off his shirt and socks and lay down on the bed, remembering the oversimple scheme which he had spoken to himself at the displaced persons' camp, the words that meant that a man had to do his duty as he saw it, and then bear the private consequences; and as part of the consequences endure a private light. 'What I didn't know was that the private consequences could hurt so!' he said. 'What I didn't know was that you have to be so all alone.' [20]

Whether the first face appears or not, the novelists' attention is focused primarily upon the process by means of which the second is converted; and the three most extended and clearest treatments of this theme are in *The Crusaders, The Naked and the Dead,* and *The Young Lions.* In each case, the novelists give us characters who are nearly, in John Aldridge's terms, "beyond the possibility of disillusion and denied even the impetus of revolt".[21] At the outset, Heym's David Yates, Mailer's Robert Hearn, and Shaw's Michael Whitacre are ideologically sterile. Intellectually, they have rejected the anarchy of the 1920's' integrity of free spirits, the doctrinaire socialism of the early depression years, and the New Deal forms of liberalism. But they have found no convictions strong enough to replace any of these. They cannot want war, as a consequence, but they cannot not want war either. Their sterility breeds cynicism, and out of this grows an individualism which stands apart from an acceptance or even a realization of its responsibilities.

But it is an individualism nonetheless, and the novelists, by exposing these characters to war, to Fascism, to death, to love – and, in the cases of Yates and Whitacre, to the first face – gradually infect the individualism with the germ of responsibility essential to the growth of value and principle, essential to involvement and commitment.

Since this aspect of *The Crusaders* was examined some chapters back, when we looked at the book as a whole, let us proceed now into *The Naked and the Dead* and *The Young Lions.*

---

[20] Loomis, *End of a War,* pp. 243-44.
[21] Aldridge, *After the Lost Generation,* pp. 118-19.

As a civilian, Robert Hearn had been rootless both physically and ideologically. He had disowned his wealthy father while a student at Harvard. He had been a moderate success as a student writer; he was a notable failure as a student Communist. After graduation, he was a moderate success as a publisher's reader, and again a notable failure as a union organizer. He succeeds in doing the things which he is apathetic about; he fails at those which he feels strongly about. He fails largely because of the strength of his feelings: he demands action from the Communists, but they want discussion; he demands that the union strike once it has been organized, but it develops that they had organized simply to keep another union out. Such situations provide good conditions for the growth of cynicism, and Hearn succumbs, returning to his wealthy family in Chicago and trying to live the life dictated by the conventions of Lake Shore Drive. This does not work either; he is at once not enough and too much the cynic to succeed in the world of carloads and contracts, high finance and wife-trading. In November, 1941, he enlists in the Army.

This action is clearly a means of escape; no convictions, no beliefs motivate it. But then Mailer juxtaposes Hearn to Cummings, and out of the clash of the uncommitted liberal intellectual and the totally committed fascist intellectual grows a Hearn newly capable of strong feelings, capable of hatred, fear, and the desire for action. After the incident of the cigarette butt, Hearn thinks:

'The only thing to do is to get by on style'. He had said that once, lived by it in the absence of anything else, and it had been a working guide, almost satisfactory until now. The only thing that had been important was to let no one in any ultimate issue ever violate integrity, and this had been an ultimate issue. Hearn felt as if an immense cyst of suppuration and purulence had burst inside him, and was infecting his bloodstream now, washing through all the conduits of his body in a sudden violent flux of change. He would have to react or die, effectively, and for one of the few times in his life he was quite uncertain of his own ability. It was impossible; he would have to do something, and he had no idea what to do.[22]

[22] Mailer, *op. cit.*, pp. 326-27.

But it is not until he is on the mountain with Croft and the Recon platoon that Hearn decides that there is hope in a struggle against all that Cummings represents; not until he is up and away from Cummings that his latent cynicism operates to help him choose meaningful action:

If you granted Cummings that man was a sonofabitch, then everything he said after that followed perfectly. The logic was inexorable.

But the history wasn't. All right, all the great dreams had blunted and turned practical and corrupt and the good things had often been done through bad motives, but still it had not all been bad, there had also been victories where there should have been defeats. The world, by all the logics, should have turned Fascist and it hadn't yet.[23]

He realizes that "if the world turned Fascist, if Cummings had his century", there would be small hope. Underground terrorism was one possibility; the concerted action of the Left – to which thought Hearn replies "Aaah, horeshit". There was also reliance on the blunder factor. One could "sit back and wait for the Fascists to louse it up". But concerted inaction is as unsatisfactory as concerted action; and both alternatives, since they argued for postponement of action, were actually dangerous: "For whatever reason, you had to keep resisting." [24]

But how is a man to resist when the opportunity for resistance is denied him? Mailer's answer is deceptively simple: he lets Hearn resolve that, on his return to headquarters, he will resign his commission. It is a small thing, insignificant, perhaps silly: "Hearn and Quixote. Bourgeois liberals." [25] It is never even put into effect, thanks to the treachery of Croft. But it is decided upon; this is the important thing. Hope rests within the individual, Mailer is saying. Constructive action begins with the individual. It is absolutely essential that each man choose rightly at each moment to do what he can do. Hearn's death signifies only that the action must not be postponed. Hearn dying is a far better man than Hearn the living dilettante; Hearn dying underlines Mailer's message imperatively.

[23]   *Ibid.*,p. 585.
[24]   *Ibid.*, p. 586.
[25]   *Ibid.*

Michael Whitacre, like Hearn, is rootless at the outset of *The Young Lions*; and like Yates, he is complacent and mentally lazy. But unlike Hearn, he is not utterly cynical; and unlike Yates, he is not given to compromising or explaining away his principles. He lacks conviction; he is so uncertain of his beliefs that he has trouble articulating them, and he is uncertain of those he can articulate. All three protagonists progress toward conviction, but Whitacre has a head start because he begins by wanting to believe.

His civilian life mirrors too closely, in its artificiality and superficiality, the world of the theater to which it is so closely bound. Whitacre is a Broadway stage manager; Laura, his wife, is an actress; their friends are playwrights, actors, directors, producers. They do not like one another, yet they gather together for gay parties; they do not love one another, yet they form adulterous alliances. "A nest of snakes hibernating for the winter", Whitacre thinks while attending one of the parties. "There was no honor to this life, no form . . . Martinis, beer, brandy, scotch, have another, and everything disappeared in a blur of alcohol – decency, fidelity, courage, decision." He sees himself: "too fat, too much liquor, too many attachments, a wife who was practically a stranger . . . doing God knows what with how many other men . . . while he frittered away the years of his youth . . . making a little money, being content, never making the bold move . . . " [26]

The restlessness behind such thoughts takes slow and inconclusive form. At a garden party, Whitacre gets into an argument with a militant pacifist who declares that the impending war (Paris is about to fall) is simply a step toward the consolidation of ruling-class power. Whitacre answers that there must be hope, that perhaps America should enter the war. " 'You want Americans to get killed too, in this swindle. . . . Is that it?' " " 'If necessary' ", Whitacre answers. " 'That's something new for you. . . . War-mongering.' " " 'It's the first time I thought of it . . . This minute.' " [27]

[26] Shaw, *The Young Lions*, p. 40.
[27] *Ibid.*, p. 98.

And the thought stays with him. At his enlistment, he turns down a chance to enter Special Services. As we have seen, he rejects the economic interpretation of the cause of the war. Later, when the party-line pacifist has become a party-line militarist demanding a second front, Whitacre refuses to sign the petition. His friends displease him greatly, he finds: "Either they were insensitively militant like Johnson the pacifist, in their untouchable civilian occupations, or, under a thin veneer of patriotism, they were cynical and resigned. And this was no time for resignation. . . . This was no time for saying no or perhaps, This was a time for great yea-saying." [28]

But Whitacre has nothing to say "yea" to. Early in his army career, he echoes loudly Arthur Miller's assertion that the American soldier would not fight and die in a property owners' war:

The orientation lectures. Military courtesy. The causes of the war which You Are Fighting. The expert on the Japanese question, a narrow, gray-faced professor from Lehigh, who had told them that it was all a question of economics. Japan needed to expand and take over the Asiatic and Pacific markets and we had to stop her and hold onto them ourselves. It was all according to the beliefs that Michael had about the causes of war for the last fifteen years. And yet, listening to the dry, professional voice, looking at the large map with spheres of influence and oil deposits and rubber plantations clearly marked out, he hated the professor, hated what he was saying. He wanted to hear that he was fighting for liberty or morality or the freedom of subject peoples, and he wanted to be told in such ringing and violent terms that he could go back to his barracks, go to the rifle range in the morning believing it.

He had wanted to say, as he thought, 'This is horrible. This is no faith to die by.' [29]

He is a willing convert, searching hungrily for a "faith to die by", and he enlists in the infantry hoping to find it there. Instead he finds that his support of a committee to send ambulances and blood banks to Spain has given him a dossier with the FBI, and will keep him out of OCS; he finds that Captain Colclough, his company commander, " 'is crazy on the subject of Reds. You'll do KP from now till we go overseas, and you'll be the first scout

[28] *Ibid.*, p. 240.
[29] *Ibid.*, p. 309.

on every advance in combat, and I wouldn't give a used condom for your chances of coming out alive' ";[30] he finds that, in the army, there is no appeal from the FBI or from the Colcloughs. But most importantly, he finds himself in the same company as Noah Ackerman, finds himself an unwilling witness of the anti-semitism climaxed by the ten merciless beatings. And because he had no firm belief to begin with, his strong desire to believe is badly shaken. Disillusioned, approaching cynicism, he uses the influence of a civilian friend to obtain a transfer to Special Services.

He goes to England in this capacity, his cynicism becoming more and more entrenched. But because he is not sufficiently politic, not respectful enough of rank, he finds himself in France as chauffeur for a Civil Affairs Colonel. Col. Pavone is a fine and sincere man woried more about the peace than about the war, seriously concerned about the present and the future of innocent civilians caught up in the invasion. Through his influence, Whitacre's cynicism melts, and he begins to feel once more the desire to act. His petitions for a transfer to the infantry are denied by Pavone on the grounds that he is needed where he is; but when the Colonel is killed, Whitacre is shipped to a Replacement Depot, marked for front-line duty.

There, he finds Noah Ackerman, who had been wounded and was waiting for reassignment. But this is a new Ackerman, sure of himself, tough, but not bitter. He has shaken off the physical and psychological effects of the beatings; through courage and conviction he has made a spot for himself in the company, and he intends to find his way back to it. Whitacre goes with him, his hope renewed, feeling that

Somewhere just ahead of him . . . under the constant trembling of the artillery among the hills, he was going to find that America he had never known on its own continent, a tortured and dying America, but an America of friends and neighbors, an America in which a man could finally put away his over-civilized doubts, his book-soured cynicism, his realistic despair, and humbly and gratefully lose himself.[31]

[30] *Ibid.*, p. 337.
[31] *Ibid.*, p. 636.

He finds it – in Noah's grief for the death of his friend, Johnny Burnecker; in Noah's willingness to teach and protect him; in Noah's and his own, physical repulsion at the anti-semitism of the liberated concentration camp inmates; in Noah's wailed hope that " 'The human beings are going to be running the world!' " [32] He finds it tragically in the death of Noah, and it becomes a conviction upon which he can and must act. Alone, disregarding the consequences, certain of the rightness of his choice to act, Whitacre commits himself finally and unalterably to the conviction and to his own responsibility to it: he stalks and kills Christian Diestl.

Noah, like Bing in *The Crusaders*, is sacrified in order that the potentially good among mankind, personified by Yates and Whitacre, may be redeemed from indifference and sent forth enlightened, apostle-like, to defeat consummate evil and to do battle with the forces of evil still prevalent among their fellow men. In *The Naked and the Dead,* the converted hero himself is sacrificed upon the same altar; it is Mailer's prayer that the reader, not simply a personification, may be the newly enlightened apostle.

At the conclusion of *The Young Lions,* as at the conclusions of *The Naked and the Dead* and *The Crusaders,* hope for the future is proffered by the authors in Hearn, Yates, and Whitacre, who voluntarily involve themselves in the fate of humanity. If Whitacre had stalked Diestl under orders, if Hearn's commission had been stripped from him – if a man takes the abuse of Queeg or allows himself to be convinced by the swollen sophistries of Col. Ross because he *must*, not because he *chooses* – then no conversion could result; then there would be no hope.

Studies in Social Psychology in World War II shows that the majority of committed soldiers were intellectuals or at least well-educated. Yates, Hearn, Whitacre – nearly all of the major characters in the novels – certainly support the point. But while the study also asserts that the law of diminishing returns operated on this commitment, that the longer the intellectual remained in the service the less committed he felt, the novelists lead their

[32]   *Ibid.*, p. 680.

characters gradually into commitment through the course of their stories. Fundamentally however, the study and the novelists are in agreement. The novelists are aware of that weakness in intellectual commitment which the study documents; they clearly believe that intellectualism plays a significant part in man's indecision or cynical lack of conviction, and they counter by applying the law of diminishing returns not to the commitment, but to the intellectualism itself. It weakens as a buttress for commitment, to be strengthened by emotionalism, something which the study did not, probably could not, measure.

This is hardly to say that the majority of the ideological novelists are anti-intellectuals, as, for example, Wouk and Cozzens are, for they find intellectualism to be unsatisfactory for almost exactly opposite reasons. While Wouk and Cozzens see it as an active danger in its challenge to the status quo, the others find it incipiently dangerous in its passively cynical tendency to accept the status quo. Nor is it to say that the novelists exalt the emotions over the intellect; they simply show that the former is necessary to the reinforcement of the latter.

The necessary first step toward voluntary involvement, they feel, is caring enough about some one or some thing to desire to be involved. The emotions must be appealed to, which in part explains why most war novels place a great deal of emphasis upon love, upon sex. There are other reasons of course: by means of sex the novelist can portray convincingly the chaotic letting down of bars that accompanies war; by means of sex he can most easily assure a good sale for his book. But the major reason in the serious novel is to shake a character out of his indifference. An indifferent man cannot accept responsibility. A man who cannot love cannot hate either, and both hate and love are basic to commitment. Put in another way: the love affairs in the serious novels help to convert the protagonists by giving them something to feel strongly about; it is then a simple matter to transfer the strength to other feelings.

Heym gives Yates Thérèse Laurent, Shaw gives Whitacre Margaret Freemantle, Burns gives the gentle and childlike Maria Rocco to Moe, a doomed Jewish infantry lieutenant oppressed by anti-semitism in *The Gallery*. Myrer, in *The Big War*, gives Newcombe Helen, whom he remembers just before he is killed, as the girl who "had freed him, even while he had thought her inferior, unworthy of him – who had healed him of his ruthless indifference. . . ." [33] Hayes gives Lisa, the girl on the Via Flaminea, to Robert so that he might have someone of his own for the short time that he is to be in Rome. When the affair is about to end, Ugo, their friend, asks Robert, " 'What will Lisa do tomorrow?' " " 'That's not my responsibility' ", Robert replies. " 'Whose is it?' " " 'Hers. God's. The world's. How do I know?' " " 'You see?' " Ugo answers; " 'it is a question of love.' " [34] And Robert learns, but too late. The novel ends as he seeks the runaway Lisa through the streets of Rome in order to fulfill the responsibility which love has awakened in him; in order to give himself.

It is possible to go on and on with examples – Boman and Daphne in *The War Lover*, for instance, and Solly Saunders and Celia, the Australian nurse, in *And Then We Heard the Thunder* – but these suffice to make the point. Hearn is one of the very few protagonists who has no one, but Mailer stresses the importance of emotional commitment as emphatically as the other novelists by a simple reversal, by showing impotence to be one of the principal factors in Cumming's intellectual Fascism, and blighted love to be at the basis of Croft's sadism.

The women in these affairs are not included among the first faces of commitment because, except in rare cases, they do not function as such. They are more passive, less argumentative; they accept the war as necessary and unavoidable, but they are not committed to it in the same way that Bing and Ackerman are. They are, in short, women, not warriors. And it is as women, as objects of sexual love, that they do their part toward converting these men who come eventually to constitute the second face.

But not only physical, sexual love is involved in caring. The

[33]   Myrer, *The Big War*, p. 393.
[34]   Hayes, *The Girl on the Via Flaminea*, p. 174.

responsibility that Yates comes to feel for Bing and Thorpe, and Whitacre for Ackerman – that responsibility upon which commitment is built – can only be called love. And more than this. There is often pervading these novels a mystical, illogical, inexplicable sense of oneness, not directed toward any individual, which motivates committed action. Col. Hobson in *And Save Them for Pallbearers*, wonders why some of his patients so willingly return to combat:

Perhaps, he thought, it is love of a sort, love that they would never understand, because it was not related to passion but a deep feeling of belonging to men they had lived with for many months. It could be a love they needed, or thought they brought to the men with whom they served, or that they wanted desperately to believe they brought those comrades.[35]

And when the doomed Danny Kantaylis in *The Big War* tells Andrea, his new wife, that he is returning to action because he believes he must, she asks him to tell her exactly what he believes in. " 'Love between people' ", he answers; " 'and the love of God. The feeling in the heart and soul. . . . That stands fast. That's the only thing they – society – can't twist around and foul up and make into something else. Everything else slithers under your feet like mud.' " " 'How do you know that?' " Andrea asks, and Danny answers: " 'I don't know. I just know it, that's all.' " [36]

It seems strange to approach the conclusion of a discussion of the ideological war novel by talking about love. One gets the feeling that an argument should be exploding here, or a bomb. But it is to love which the novelists ultimately direct our attention; love as a motivation for sacrifice; love as pure emotion resulting in sex. Love as the parent of that sense of responsibility which grows in the uncommitted or weakly committed intellectual until it becomes a realization then a conviction that every man is at once island and not island, that every man who stands alone

---

[35] James Garrett, *And Save Them for Pallbearers*, pp. 257-58.
[36] Myrer, *op. cit.*, p. 69.

stands necessarily not alone, that the bell tolls for each and all if it tolls for one.

Then and only then, the ideological novelists feel, can Fascism – whenever and whenever it appears, under whatever name, in whatever guise – be defeated and destroyed.

VII. CONCLUSION

The ideological war novel was at once an end and a beginning. It was the culmination of that sort of social critical realism which was so influential in American letters during the first third of this century, and which dominated the literature of the 1930's. All of the social evils and ills of those years had been accumulated and magnified by the novelists in Nazi-Fascism, and when it was defeated, and their novels concerned with its defeat were written, their crusading impulse abated sharply. Few of them took up the gauntlet thrown by the extreme Right in the late 1940's and early '50's. Irwin Shaw attacked the witch hunt in *The Troubled Air*, a novel about the black list of suspected Communist sympathizers in the entertainment industry – a story strangely but somehow appropriately dated by the fact that, in those blossoming days of television, it was concerned with radio. Stefan Heym produced a 1930's type of protest novel called *Goldsborough,* a story about the coal mine strikes of 1946 and 1949. The title of the novel is the name of a fictitious town in Pennsylvania, but significantly to Heym's attitude toward the strikes, it is also the name of the Federal Judge who issued the injunction against the 1949 strike, who declared failure to obey the injunction to be anarchy, and who consequently fined the United Mine Workers $3,500,000 for contempt of his court. And Norman Mailer made his first sojourn away from fiction writing and into politics in 1948, joining battle with the League of Omnipotent Men by actively supporting Henry Wallace, candidate for president on the Progressive Party ticket.

But when Mailer spoke again in fiction, what he said came

out as *Barbary Shore,* a novel which reflected the mind of the liberal anti-Fascist intellectual ex-war novelist more clearly than any protest novel could have in 1951. It is a novel concerned with the death of the socialist dream as it had been dreamt in the 1930's. It had been killed by Stalinism and by the Cold War fear that the button might be pushed at any instant by either side opening the doors to nightmare. Nothing could have brought it back, neither the resurgence of a now warped and impotent Trotskyism nor the insidious charges of the extreme Right. All that was left was a faint hope, little more than a gleam, clutched by an amnesiac victim-veteran of the war, whose face has been so changed by plastic surgery that he cannot recognise himself in the mirror, and most of whose memories – even those flitting and episodic – are of himself as a revolutionary socialist embroiled in what is obviously 1930's strike activity.

Barbary Shore clearly shows that the crusading optimism of the 1930's and of the war years has ended. Being opposed to the neo-Fascism of McCarthyism is not the same as opposing Hitler, nor is it the same as committing oneself to the crusade. New causes, new positive positions to balance the negation of anti-McCarthyism were needed. They were not to come until the 1960's and the opening of the Civil Rights struggle. But the war novelists themselves, in their insistence upon the dignity of the individual, in their charge that even American society, in Emerson's words, "everywhere is in conspiracy against the manhood of every one of its members", prefigure that struggle. *And Then We Heard the Thunder,* for example, is a novel at least as much about the Negroes' battle against racism as it is about the war. And it is significant that it appeared in the same year (1960) as James Baldwin's *Another Country*.

But it is not only in terms of the revived social criticism attending the Civil Rights struggle that the ideological war novelists mark the beginning of something. Their emphasis upon individualism, responsibility, commitment, upon the terrible anxiety of the necessity of choice, their voluntary submission to the paradox of collective individualism, leads them to the threshold of existentialism, the philosophy which continues to grip the creative imagination more forcefully than any other. They do not cross the threshold, though occasionally they come perilously close to it – witness the anguished cry of the guilt-ridden Leggett who is faced with the choice of accepting or rejecting responsibility for having blindly chosen to participate in the war: " 'What I didn't know was that the private consequences could hurt so! . . . What I didn't know was that you had to be so all alone.' " [1] The philosophy is logical and unified, complete with philosophers and apostles, with dialectic and with answers. Significantly, it experienced its modern (i.e. Sartean) impetus in war-time France, growing out of chaos, out of a need to rebuild a society which had capitulated its dignity and pride. At the time existentialism rose, the United States was a strong, self-assured nation, dangerously in need of an examination of conscience and of reform, but hardly in need of rebuilding. The thinking of the war novelists paralleled that of the existentialists, but remained unformalized, a mixture of philosophy and social criticism held together by the facts of war and Fascism. The novelists' attention is fastened upon the presentness and urgency of the war, and upon the ominous reality of the essential evil which they believed was its cause. Their individuals are those who have been affected by the war; their anxiety is bounded and limited by the desire on the one hand to ameliorate its cause, and on the other, by the hope that it may eventually be destroyed utterly. The resolution of the paradox however, for both the war novelists and the existentialists – in spite of the war novelists' belief in essential evil and essential good, in spite of their particularized rather than universalized anxiety, in spite of their acceptance of the necessity of collective action – is individual commitment and involvement.

Though the necessity of collectivism ended with the defeat of Nazi-Fascism, the conviction of individual responsibility for individual human action persisted. It pervades the work of the post-war writers, of Bellow and Styron and Malamud, for example, and of the later Mailer and Edward Loomis, who seem indeed finally to have crossed the threshold of existentialism in *An American Dream* and *The Charcoal Horse* respectively. This

[1] Loomis, *End of a War*, p. 244.

is not to say that these novelists are at all directly indebted to the war novelists for their ideas or their convictions; it is to say that they are writing within a tradition to which the war novelists contributed a substantial basis. Also within that tradition are the absurdists or black humorists who have risen to prominence in the years since the war. Their emphasis upon failure of communication among men, upon life as a series of comic interruptions interspersed with moments of comic clarity, or vice-versa, is really an almost excessive emphasis upon individualism. What remains after communication breaks down and the interruptions multiply is the individual himself, perhaps existential, perhaps not, but certainly alone. His condition is absurd because the world which surrounds him and the self inside him renders him incapable of coping with the responsibility to and for himself which his aloneness has thrust upon him; and his attempts to do so – abortive, pitiful, preposterous – are ultimately comic.

Joseph Heller's *Catch-22*, an important war novel which has not as yet figured in this discussion, becomes a key book at this point, for it is the one novel which attempts to treat the war as absurd. It proceeds from Heller's discovery that everything in the modern world is up for grabs; that nothing – and therefore, ipso facto, everything – makes coherent, logical sense. By the ancient comic device of portraying the preposterous as normal, it is possible to make of this discovery something delightfully, often uproariously funny, and Heller is superb at the creation of this kind of comedy.

Nearly everything and everybody in *Catch-22* is outlandish, whacky. There is Lt. Scheisskopf whose monomaniacal love for dress parades finally earns him promotion to General. There is ex-PFC Wintergreen who, for all practical purposes, runs the war from his clerk's desk by manipulating orders and memoranda. There is the Major named Major Major Major who got his rank through an understandable IBM error, who doesn't want the rank nor know how to use it, and who consequently flees his office through a window whenever he is about to be approached with a problem. And there are others, equally whacky, but in a far more vicious, deadly sense: There is Captain Black who, out of jealousy of Major Major, institutes the Glorius Loyalty Oath Crusade in order to prove that Major Major is a Communist by the simple device of refusing to let him sign the Oath ("'You never heard him denying it until we began accusing him, did you?'").[2] There is Col. Cathcart who is most upset to learn that enlisted men pray to the same God as officers (recall the famous Mauldin cartoon of the sunset?) and that God listens to them; whose one great dream is to be immortalized in a feature story in the *Saturday Evening Post*, and who, to achieve this end, keeps raising the number of missions his squadron must fly until he has tripled the required number. There is Cpl. Whitcomb, the Chaplain's assistant, who devises a form letter to take care of the growing casualties resulting from Col. Cathcart's policy; the letter reads in part: "Dear Mrs., Mr., Miss, or Mr. and Mrs.: Words cannot express the deep personal grief I experienced when your husband, son, father, or brother was killed, wounded, or reported missing in action."[3] And finally – though there are many others who could and some readers would argue should be mentioned – there is Milo Minderbinder, angle-shooter extraordinary, caricature of the American businessman. He forms a syndicate, M & M Enterprises, dealing in everything imaginable from Lebanese cedar to Dutch tulips, Swiss cheeses, Spanish oranges, and Egyptian cotton. He insists that he operates a legitimate business in the American way, for each member of the squadron is a shareholder in the syndicate; and, since business is above quarrels between nations, there are English, French, German, and Italian partners in the syndicate as well – all of which makes very little difference since the profits are all plowed back into the business anyway, and there are no holds to share. Milo sells petroleum and ball bearings to the Germans and even contracts with them, in a major coup for the syndicate, to bomb and strafe his own airfield with planes of its own squadron. And because he is successful in the American tradition – that is, because his books show a substantial profit – Milo is admired and respected by the American people; even, though somewhat grudg-

---

[2]   Joseph Heller, *Catch-22*, p. 113.
[3]   *Ibid.*, p. 275.

ingly, by those who lost loved ones in the bombing and strafing.

Lt. John Yossarian, a bomber pilot from whose point of view we observe most of the action, is one of the few even moderately "normal" characters in the novel. The others – the Chaplain, Doc Daneeka, Major Danby, each a friend and confidant of Yossarian – are all caught up to some degree in the prevailing absurdity. But Yossarian is not. Each of his actions, preposterous, indeed crazy though it might be, is carefully calculated both to protest the absurdity and to get him out of combat if not clean out of the service. He complains of a non-existent liver pain in order to be hospitalized to await the pains becoming jaundice so that it can be treated (the first variation of the elaborate joke upon which the novel is built: the doctors can cure jaundice, but a simple pain in the liver they cannot cure, whether the pain exists or not). He censors enlisted men's mail by editing the letters unmercifully, sometimes deleting all modifiers and articles, sometimes blacking out all but the saluation and close; and he signs as the name of the censoring officer either Washington Irving or Irving Washington. He either goes to sleep or behaves boorishly at briefing sessions. On the day that he is to be awarded a medal he appears in ranks totally nude, protesting that his uniform is covered with the blood of the man whose death earned him the medal. But his counter absurdity campaign is fruitless, the world being what it is. In the first place, Yossarian is not considered crazy by his superiors but simply insubordinate, and therefore eligible not for a Section-8, but for flying more combat missions. In the second place, there is the magnificently absurd logic of Catch-22 "which specified that a concern for one's own safety in the face of dangers that were real and immediate was the process of a rational mind". All one must do to be grounded for mental reasons, Doc Daneeka explains to Yossarian, is to ask; but asking is proof that one is not crazy. Put in another way: "If he flew [more missions] he was crazy and didn't have to; but if he didn't want to he was sane and had to." [4]

The novel moves by fits and starts toward Yossarian's even-

---

[4] *Ibid.*, p. 46.

tual desertion, but this is not a forward movement. It really does not go anywhere that it has not already been in its first few pages, albeit with slight variations in situation and character. In addition, there is no clearly juxtapositional relationship among its episodes; they are by and large interchangeable – so much so that many of them could actually be removed without marring the novel structurally at all. In fact, since Heller tends to tell the same joke and laugh the same ironic laugh over and over again, the removal of some of the episodes could cut down the repetitiveness, the redundancy, and improve the novel considerably. Plotless really, the book is unified by the pattern of absurdity established at its outset. But this is a tenuous unity at best; and it is here, faced with chaotic structure and endless repetition of episodes which individually are often quite funny, that one begins to feel doubt and dissatisfaction about the novel. Somehow, one feels, it would have been better if it had been better made.

In one sense, this criticism may seem rather picayune; after all, the novel remains brilliantly comic, episodic or not. But in another, higher sense, the criticism is of major seriousness, for the episodic flaw is symptomatic of the novel's failure – and most importantly, of its failure on its own terms: as absurd. Perhaps paradoxically, the successful portrayal of absurdity, because it requires a tightness rather than a looseness of form, also requires argument, the positing of directions from which and toward which and around which the action and the characters may move – requires if you will at least the potential existence of the Court or the Castle or Godot or the rhinocerous or an American Dream. The artist must have a position, a point of view, some awareness of what things should or could be in order to be aware of the absurdity of things as they are.

Heller either lacks this awareness, or he prefers to focus upon the merely comic which is the inherent quality of the absurd. Milo Minderbinder is a case in point. This soldier-businessman who profits so heavily from the non-sense of war could have been made to crystallize war's absurdity, but he remains little more than a slapstick caricature whose exploits are too preposterous and overdrawn and directionless to be much more than burlesque blackouts. By the same token, Milo could have been turned into an ideological villain like Willoughby or Loomis. The anonymous reviewer of the novel for *Daedalus* (whose review was reprinted as a feature in the *National Observer*) seems to believe that this was Heller's intention: "*Catch-22* is immoral", he writes, "because it follows a fashion in spitting indiscriminately at business and the professions, at respectability, at ideals, at all visible tokens of superiority. It is a leveling book in the worst sense, leveling everything and everyone downward." [5]

It takes a very perceptive reader indeed to find in Milo any representation of social criticism, let alone the leftist-nihilism suggested in the review. The evidence in fact would seem as justifiably to indicate that Heller is conservative, that by means of reducing Milo to the ridicule of caricature, he has reduced social criticism itself, especially of businessmen, to the same level. To Heller's credit, neither interpretation is acceptable. Milo may be disappointing as an absurd foil because he is too comic, but at least he is consistently comic, and no social critical foil either.

What *Catch-22* appears to be then is a not-too-serious anti-war novel – and serious or not, as such it would be a unique phenomenon within the literature of World War II. But appearances are deceptive; in this case, they apparently even deceived Heller. For in the final pages of the novel, he invests Yossarian with a totally unexpected idealism. In a scene between Yossarian and his friend Major Danby – a scene recognized even by Robert Brustein in his extremely favorable review as "an inspirational sequence which is the weakest thing in the book" [6] – Yossarian justifies his imminent desertion against an appeal to his patriotism and his anti-Nazi conscience. " 'This is not World War One' ", Danby says. " 'You must never forget that we're at war with aggressors who would not let either one of us live if they won.' " " 'I know that' ", Yossarian replies. " 'Christ, Danby, I earned that medal I got, no matter what their reasons were for giving it to me. I've flown seventy goddam combat missions. Don't talk

[5] *The National Observer* (February 18, 1963), p. 14.
[6] Robert Brustein, "The Logic of Survival in a Lunatic World", *The New Republic* (November 13, 1961), p. 13.

to me about fighting to save my country. I've been fighting all along to save my country. . . . The Germans will be beaten in a few months. And Japan will be beaten a few months after that. If I were to give up my life now, it wouldn't be for my country.' " [7]

The scene comes as a shocking surprise. It represents a reversal of intention almost as flagrant as Wouk's in *The Caine Mutiny*. There is nothing wrong with an American novelist being in favor of the war; Heller would in fact, as suggested above, be unique if he opposed it. But since he appears to be opposed to it throughout the novel, there is something wrong with Yossarian, his victim-spokesman, expressing pro-war sentiments, weak and unconvincing though they might be. One might forgive the sequence if he could see it as even moderately integral, if the novel had prepared the way for it. But such is not the case; the sequence is not added up to, it is simply added on. Heller retreats from the seriousness of both social criticism and absurdity for 435 pages and then, as if in afterthought, seems to say: 'You see? This has all been a joke – good, clean fun with overtones of the macabre to titilate. But underneath, there has really been something deep and important going on.' Unfortunately however, there hasn't been.

Despite its failings, or perhaps because of them, *Catch-22* is nearly the perfect war novel to round off this discussion. It is in itself both that end and beginning referred to at the outset of this chapter. It is a transition piece, looking backward to the war novels which portrayed war as barbaric but argued that this war was necessary, and forward to those post-war disaffiliates who portrayed the chaos of a world without convictions and values, and laughed at it. The novel's weakness grows out of Heller's inability to make up his mind whether he is an ideological war novelist, an anti-war novelist, or an *avant-garde* absurdist. But for our purposes, that weakness is a virtue for it helps us to comprehend once more most clearly the intellectual and emotional soul-searching which preceded the ideological novelists' commitment to the crusade, and to understand finally and fully the strength of that commitment.

[7] *Catch-22*, pp. 435-36.

BIBLIOGRAPHY

The first part of this bibliography, labeled "Sources", is a selected list of the books and articles which bear upon the subject of this discussion. It includes the non-World War II materials, fiction, drama, and essays, which have been mentioned here and there in the book. The second part of the bibliography, "World War II Novels", is as complete a list of World War II novels written by Americans concerning Americans in the uniforms of any Allied power as I could compile. It is complete through mid-1966.

I should like to thank Henry Koch and the Michigan State University Library, and Richard Close, for their cooperation and assistance in making the bibliography as complete as possible.

SOURCES

"A Look at Catch-22", *The National Observer*, February 18, 1963, 14.

Aldridge, John W., *After the Lost Generation* (New York, McGraw Hill Book Company, Inc., 1951).

Allen, Frederick Lewis, *Only Yesterday* (New York, Harper and Brothers, 1931).

——, *Since Yesterday* (New York, Harper and Brothers, 1940).

Barck, Oscar T., Jr., *A History of the United States Since 1945* (New York, Dell Publishing Company, 1965).

Beach, Joseph Warren, *American Fiction: 1920-1940* (New York, Macmillan Company, 1941).

Bittner, William, "Schweik Among the Herrenvolk", *The Nation*, CLXXIV (June 22, 1957), 550-52.

Boyd, Thomas, *Through the Wheat* (New York, Charles Scribner's Sons, 1923).

Brustein, Robert, "The Logic of Survival in a Lunatic World", *The New Republic*, November 13, 1961, 11-13.

Cobb, Humphrey, *Paths of Glory* (New York, The Viking Press, 1935).

Congdon, Don, editor, *Combat: European Theater* (New York, Dell Publishing Company, Inc., 1958).

——, *Combat: Pacific Theater* (New York, Dell Publishing Company, Inc.. 1958).

Cowley, Malcolm, *Exile's Return* (New York, The Viking Press, 1951).

——, *The Literary Situation* (New York, The Viking Press, 1954).

——, Review of *By Love Possessed, New York Times Book Review*, LXII (August 25, 1957), 1.

Critoph, Gerald E., "The American Literary Reaction to World War I", unpublished Ph.D. Dissertation in American Civilization, University of Pennsylvania, 1957.

Dos Passos, John, *Three Soldiers* (The Modern Library) (New York, Random House, 1932).

——, *USA*, 3 vols. (The Modern Library) (New York, Random House, 1937).

Eisinger, Chester E., *Fiction of the Forties* (Chicago, University of Chicago Press, 1963).

Farrell, James T., *My Days of Anger* (New York, The Vanguard Press, 1943).

——, *The Studs Lonigan Trilogy* (New York, The Vanguard Press, 1944).

Feigenbaum, Lawrence H., *War, as Viewed by Postwar Novelists, World Wars 1 and II*. Ann Arbor (Mich.), University Microfilms, Microfilm AC-1 # 2181 (New York University, 1950).

Fein, Richard J., "Major American Poetry of World War II", unpublished Ph.D. Dissertation, New York University, 1960.

Fenton, Charles A., "Introduction" to *Best Short Stories of World War II* (New York, The Viking Press, 1957).

Frederick, John T., "Fiction of the Second World War", *College English*, XVII (January 17, 1956), 197-204.

Frohock, W. M., *The Novel of Violence in America* (Dallas, Southern Methodist University Press, 1950).

Geismar, Maxwell, *Writers in Crisis* (London, Secker & Warburg, 1947).

Halprin, Lee S., "American Liberalism, Literature, and World War II", *Minnesota Review*, III (Winter, 1963), 179-92.

Hemingway, Ernest, *A Farewell to Arms* (New York, Charles Scribner's Sons, 1929).

——, *For Whom the Bell Tolls* (New York, Charles Scribner's Sons, 1944).

Hoffman, Frederick J., *The Modern Novel in America* (Chicago, Regnery, 1951).

——, *The Twenties* (New York, The Viking Press, 1955).

Howe, Irving, *Politics and the Novel* (New York, Horizon Press, Inc., 1957).

Ickes, Harold L., *The Lowering Clouds* (New York, Simon and Schuster, 1954).

Johnson, Gerald W., *Incredible Tale* (New York, Harper and Brothers, 1950).

Kahn, Luther, "The German War Novel", *Trace*, January-February, 1960, 19-24.

Kazin, Alfred, *On Native Grounds* (New York, Reynal & Hitchcock, 1942).

Leary, Lewis G., *Articles on American Literature: 1900-1950* (Durham [N. C.], Duke University Press, 1954).

Leighton, Isabel, editor, *The Aspirin Age: 1919-1941* (New York, Simon and Schuster, 1949).

Mailer, Norman, *Cannibals and Christians* (New York, Dial Press, 1966).
March, William, *Company K.* (American Century Series) (New York, Sagamore Press, 1957).
Oldsey, Bernard S., *Aspects of Combat in the Novel, 1900-1950.* Ann Arbor (Mich.), University Microfilms. Microfilm # 14,871 (Penn State University, 1955).
Remarque, Erich Maria. *All Quiet on the Western Front* (London, G. P. Putnam's Sons, 1929).
Rideout, Walter B., *The Radical Novel in the United States* (Cambridge [Mass.], Harvard University Press, 1956).
Schlesinger, Arthur M., Jr., *The Coming of the New Deal* (Vol. II of *The Age of Roosevelt*) (Boston, Houghton Mifflin Co., 1958).
——, *The Crisis of the Old Order* (Vol. I of *The Age of Roosevelt*) (Boston, Houghton Mifflin Co., 1957).
——, "A Memorandum to the Democratic Party", *The Detroit News* (August 10, 11, 1959).
Shaw, Irwin, *The Assassin* (New York, Random House, 1946).
——, *Bury the Dead* (New York, Random House, 1936).
Smitter, Wessel, *F.O.B. Detroit* (New York, Harper and Brothers, 1938).
Steinbeck, John, *The Grapes of Wrath* (New York, The Viking Press, 1939).
——, *In Dubious Battle* (New York, The Viking Press, 1936).
——, *The Moon Is Down* (New York, The Viking Press, 1942).
Studies in Social Psychology in World War II, 4 vols. (Princeton, University of Princeton Press, 1955).
Sutton, Horace, "Defeatism in Contemporary Literature", *The Saturday Review*, XXXIX (December 29, 1956), 20.
Trumbo, Dalton, *Johnny Got His Gun* (New York, J. B. Lippincott Co., 1939).
Van Doren, Carl, *The American Novel* (New York, The Macmillan Co., 1940).
Waite, John, "The Masses: A Study in American Rebellion", unpublished Doctoral Dissertation (American Civilization, University of Maryland, 1951).
Waldmeir, Joseph J., "Novelists of Two Wars", *The Nation*, CLXXXVII (November 1, 1958), 304-07.
Wright, Richard, *Native Son* (New York, Harper and Brothers, 1941).

WORLD WAR II NOVELS

Abrahams, William, *Interval in Carolina* (New York, Simon and Schuster, 1945).
Ageton, Arthur A., *The Jungle Seas* (New York, Random House, 1954).
Andersen, U. S., *The Smoldering Sea* (New York, A. A. Wyn, Inc., 1953).
Appel, Benjamin, *Fortress in the Rice* (Indianapolis [Ind.], Bobbs-Merrill, 1951).
——, *Plunder* (Greenwich [Conn.], Fawcett Publications, Inc., 1952).

Archambault, Alberie A., *The Samsons* (Boston, B. Humphries, Inc., 1941).

Ardrey, Robert, *Worlds Beginning* (New York, Duell, Sloan, & Pearce, 1944).

Arnold, Elliott, *The Commandos* (New York, Duell, Sloan, & Pearce, 1942).

——, *Tomorrow will Sing* (New York, Duell, Sloan, & Pearce, 1945).

Ashmead, John, *The Mountain* (Boston, Houghton Mifflin Co., 1961).

Atwell, Lester, *Private* (New York, Simon and Schuster, 1958).

Bagnall, Stephen, *The Crater's Edge* (New York, William Morrow and Co., 1946).

Baltis, George A., *The Orphans of Singapore* (Los Angeles, Privately published by G. A. Baltis, 1943).

Barr, George, *Epitaph for an Enemy* (New York, Harper and Brothers, 1958).

Barrington, Lowell, *The Deserter* (New York, The Macmillan Co., 1954).

Beach, Edward L., *Run Silent, Run Deep* (New York, Henry Holt and Co., Inc., 1955).

Bellah, James W., *Ward Twenty* (Garden City [N. Y.], Doubleday and Company, 1946).

Bergamini, David, *The Fleet in the Window* (New York, Simon and Schuster, 1960).

Berkowitz, Henry J., *Boot Camp* (Philadelphia [Pa.], Jewish Publishing Society of America, 1948).

Bernstein, Alec, *From the City, From the Plough* (New York, I. Washburn, 1949).

Blanchard, Henry, *The White Bull* (Garden City [N. Y.], Doubleday and Company, 1947).

Blum, Ralph, *The Foreigner* (New York, Athaneum, 1961).

Blunden, Godfrey, *The Time of the Assassins* (Philadelphia [Pa.], J. B. Lippincott Co., 1952).

Booth, Fred W., *Victory Also Ends* (New York, Rinehart & Co., Inc., 1952).

Bourjaily, Vance, *End of My Life* (New York, Bantam Books, Inc., 1952).

Bowman, Peter, *Beach Red* (New York, Random House, 1945).

Boyd, Dean, *Lighter Than Air* (New York, Harcourt, Brace & Company, 1961).

Boyden, Frederick, *The Hospital* (New York, Farrar, Straus & Cudahy, 1951).

Brelis, Dean, *The Mission* (New York, Random House, 1958).

Brennan, Dan, *Never So Young Again* (New York, Rinehart & Co., Inc., 1946).

Brier, Royce, *Last Boat from Beyrouth* (New York, D. Appleton-Century Company, 1943).

Brinkley, William, *Don't Go Near the Water* (New York, Random House, 1956).

——, *The Ninety and Nine* (New York, Doubleday and Company, 1966).

——, *Quicksand* (New York, E. P. Dutton, 1948).

Brittain, Very Mary, *Born 1925: A Novel of Youth* (New York, Macmillan Co., 1949).

Brooks, Richard, *The Brick Foxhole* (New York, Harper and Brothers, 1945).
Brophy, John, *Spearhead* (New York, Harper and Brothers, 1943).
Brown, Harry, *A Walk in the Sun* (New York, A. A. Knopf, 1944).
Brown, Joe D., *Kings Go Forth* (New York, William Morrow and Co., 1956).
Buckley, David, *Pride of Innocence* (New York, Henry Holt and Co., Inc., 1957).
Burgess, Jackson, *The Atrocity* (New York, G. P. Putnam's Sons, 1961).
Burnet, Dana, *The Pool* (New York, A. A. Knopf, 1945).
Burns, John Horne, *The Gallery* (New York, Harper and Brothers, 1947).
Busch, Niven, *They Dream of Home* (New York, O. Appleton-Century Company, 1944).
Butler, Charles, *Follow Me Ever* (New York, Pantheon Books, 1951).
Byrd, Sam, *Hurry Home to My Heart* (New York, Houghton Mifflin Co., 1945).
Calmer, Ned, *The Strange Land* (New York, Charles Scribner's Sons, 1950).
Camerer, David M., *The Damned Wear Wings* (New York, Doubleday and Company, 1958).
Carmer, Carl, *The Jesse James of the Java Sea* (New York, Farrar & Rinehart, Inc., 1945).
Chamales, T. Tom, *Never So Few* (New York, Charles Scribner's Sons, 1957).
Chambliss, William C., *Boomerang* (New York, Harcourt, Brace & Company, 1944).
Chevalier, Haakon M., *The Man Who Would Be God* (New York, G. P. Putnam's Sons, 1959).
Clagett, John, *The Slot* (New York, Crown Publishers, 1958).
Clavell, James, *King Rat* (Boston, Little, Brown, 1962).
Cochrell, Boyd, *Barren Beaches of Hell* (New York, Henry Bolt and Co., 1959).
Coleman, Lonnie, *Time Moving West* (New York, E. P. Dutton, 1947).
——, *Ship's Company* (New York, Dell Publishing Co., Inc., 1955).
Connell, Evan S., *The Patriot* (New York, The Viking Press, 1960).
Cook, Canfield, *Secret Mission* (New York, Grosset & Dunlop, 1943).
——, *Springboard to Tokyo* (New York, Grosset & Dunlop, 1943).
Cooper, Brian, *Giselle* (New York, The Vanguard Press, 1958).
——, *Maria* (New York, The Vanguard Press, 1955).
Cooper, Herston, *Over My Shoulder* (Philadelphia [Pa.], Dorrance & Co., Inc., 1943).
Cooper, J. C., *The Gesture* (New York, Harper and Brothers, 1948).
Cooper, Lettice U., *Black Bethlehem* (New York, The Macmillan Co., 1947).
Coyle, Kathleen, *To Hold Against Famine* (New York, E. P. Dutton, 1942).
Cozzens, James G., *Guard of Honor* (New York, Harcourt, Brace & Company, 1948).

Crockett, Lucy H., *The Magnificent Bastards* (New York, Farrar, Straus & Cudahy, 1954).

Dahl, Ronald, *Over to You* (New York, Reynal & Hitchcock, 1945).

Dale, Celia, *The Least of These* (New York, The Macmillan Co., 1944).

Dednon, Emmett, *Duty to Live* (Boston [Mass.], Houghton Mifflin Co., 1946).

De Pereda, Prudencio, *All the Girls We Loved* (New York, Signet Books, 1948).

DeVries, Robert, *Gala Day* (New York, The Vanguard Press, 1954).

Dibner, Martin, *The Deep Six* (New York, Permabooks, 1955).

Dodson, Kenneth, *Away All Boats* (Boston [Mass.], Little, Brown, 1954).

Downes, Donald C., *Orders to Kill* (New York, Rinehart & Co., 1958).

Downey, Fairfax D., *Jezebel the Jeep* (New York, Dodd, Mead & Company, 1944).

Dunsany, Edward, *Guerrilla* (New York, Bobbs-Merrill, 1944).

Eastlake, William, *Castle Keep* (New York, Simon and Schuster, 1965).

Edgar, Louise E., *Out of Bounds* (Philadelphia [Pa.], Dorrance & Co., Inc., 1950).

Edmiston, James, *Home Again* (Garden City [N. Y.], Doubleday and Company, 1955).

Anonymous, *Escape from Konigstein* (New York, Charles Scribner's Sons, 1944).

Ethridge, Willie, *This Little Pig Stayed Home* (New York, The Vanguard Press, 1944).

Eyster, Warren, *Far from the Customary Skies* (New York, Random House, 1953).

Falstein, Louis, *Face of a Hero* (New York, Harcourt, Brace & Company, 1950).

Ferris, Bert R., *Restless Road* (Boston, Houghton Mifflin Co., 1946).

Fields, Arthur C., *World Without Heroes* (New York, McGraw Hill, 1950).

Fisher, Phillip M., *Vanishing Ships* (New York, M. S. Mill Co., Inc., 1943).

Fosburgh, H., *View from the Air* (New York, M. S. Mill Co., Inc., 1943).

Frank, Pat., *An Affair of State* (New York, J. B. Lippincott Co., 1948).

Freedman, Ralph, *Divided* (New York, E. P. Dutton, 1948).

Freeman, Walter, *The Last Blitzkrieg* (New York, Signet Books, 1958).

Fridley, William, *A Time to go Home* (New York, E. P. Dutton, 1951).

Frizell, Bernard, *Ten Days in August* (New York, Simon and Schuster, Inc., 1956).

Fuller, Robert G., *Danger! Marines at Work* (New York, Random House, 1959).

Gabriel, Gilbert W., *Love from London* (New York, The Macmillan Co., 1946).

Gallico, Paul, *The Lonely* (New York, A. A. Knopf, 1950).

Garrett, James, *And Save them for Pallbearers* (New York, Julian Messner, Inc., 1958).

Garth, David, *Watch on the Bridge* (New York, G. P. Putnam's Sons, 1959).

Geer, Andrew C., *The Sea Chase* (New York, Harper and Brothers, 1948).

Gellhorn, Martha, *Wine of Astonishment* (New York, Charles Scribner's Sons, 1948).
Gibbs, Arthur H., *Way of Life* (Boston [Mass.], Little, Brown, 1947).
Gidding, Nelson, *End Over End* (New York, The Viking Press, 1946).
Gies, Joseph, *They Never Had it so Good* (New York, Harper and Brothers, 1949).
Gilbert, Michael, *The Danger Within* (New York, Harper and Brothers, 1952).
Gilpatric, Guy, *Action in the North Atlantic* (New York, E. P. Dutton, 1943).
Giovannitti, Len., *The Prisoners of Combine D* (New York, Henry Holt and Company, Inc., 1957).
Goertz, Arthmise, *Dream of Fuji* (New York, McGraw Hill, 1958).
Goethals, Thomas, *Chains of Command* (New York, Random House, 1955).
Goldsmith, Martin M., *Shadows at Noon* (Chicago, Ziff-Davis Publishing Co., 1943).
Goodman, Mitchell, *The End of It* (New York, Horizon Press, 1961).
Goran, Lester, *Maria Light* (Boston, Houghton Mifflin Co., 1962).
Greenfield, George C., *Desert Episode* (New York, Macmillan Co., 1945).
Grove, Walt, *Down* (New York, Dell Publishing Co., 1953).
Guerard, Albert, *Night Journey* (New York, Alfred A. Knopf, 1950).
Gwaltney, Francis I., *The Day the Century Ended* (New York, Rinehart & Co., Inc., 1955).
Haines, William W., *Command Decision* (Boston [Mass.], Little, Brown, 1947).
Hall, James N., *Lost Island* (Boston [Mass.], Little, Brown, 1944).
Hall, Warner, *Even Jericho* (Philadelphia [Pa.], Macrae-Smith Company, 1944).
Hallet, Richard M., *Foothold of Earth* (Garden City [N. Y.], Doubleday, Doran and Company, Inc., 1944).
Hardison, Irene, *Nightingale in the Jungle* (Philadelphia [Pa.], Dorrance & Co., Inc., 1954).
Harper, Frank, *Night Climb* (New York, Longmans, Green & Co., 1946).
Harr, Bill, *Combat Boots* (New York, Exposition Press Inc., 1952).
Hawkes, John, *The Cannibal* (Norfolk [Conn.], New Directions, 1949).
——, "The Owl", in *The Goose on the Grave and The Owl* (Norfolk [Conn.], New Directions, 1954).
Hayes, Alfred, *All Thy Conquests* (New York, Howell, Soskin, 1946).
——, *The Girl on the Via Flaminea* (New York, Harper and Brothers, 1949).
Heatter, Basil, *The Captain's Lady* (New York, Farrar, Straus & Cudahy, 1950).
——, *The Dim View* (New York, Farrar, Straus & Cudahy, 1949).
Heggen, Thomas, *Mister Roberts* (Boston [Mass.], Houghton Mifflin Co., 1946).
Heller, Joseph, *Catch-22* (New York, Simon and Schuster, 1961).
Helm, Stephens, *Blood in the Dust* (New York, Exposition Press, Inc., 1953).

Hendricks, Earl, *Kriegie's Journey* (New York, Exposition Press, Inc., 1955).
Herber, William, *Tomorrow to Live* (New York, Coward-McCann, 1957).
Hersey, John R., *A Bell for Adano* (New York, A. A. Knopf, 1944).
——, *The War Lover* (New York, A. A. Knopf, 1959).
Heym, Stefan, *The Crusaders* (Boston [Mass.], Little, Brown, 1948).
Hill, Grace, *Time of the Singing Birds* (New York, J. B. Lippincott Co., 1944).
Hoellering, Franz, *Furlough* (New York, The Viking Press, 1944).
Hoffman, William, *The Trumpet Unblown* (Crest Books) (New York, Fawcett World Library, 1957).
——, *Yancey's War* (New York, Doubleday and Company, 1966).
Horwitz, Julius, *Can I Get There by Candlelight?* (New York, Athaneum, 1964).
Howe, George L., *Call it Treason* (New York, The Viking Press, 1949).
Hubler, Richard G., *I've Got Mine* (New York, G. P. Putnam's Sons, 1946).
Huie, William B., *Americanization of Emily* (New York, E. P. Dutton, 1959).
Humes, H. L., *Underground City* (New York, Random House, 1958).
Hunt, G., *Coral Comes High* (New York, Harper and Brothers, 1957).
Hunt, Howard, *East of Farewell* (New York, A. A. Knopf, 1942).
——, *Limit of Darkness* (New York, Random House, 1944).
Husted, Richard L., *Replacement* (Boston [Mass.], Meador Publishing Co., 1948).
Hutchens, Paul, *Undefeated* (Chicago, Moody Press, 1945).
Hutchinson, R. C., *Interim* (New York, Rinehart & Co., Inc., 1945).
Hyman, Mac., *No Time for Sergeants* (New York, Random House, 1954).
Ingersoll, Ralph M., *Wine of Violence* (New York, Farrar, Straus & Young, 1951).
Jenks, Almet, *The Second Chance* (Philadelphia [Pa.], J. B. Lippincott Co., 1958).
Jonas, Carl, *Beachhead on the Wind* (Boston [Mass.], Little, Brown, 1945).
Jones, James, *From Here to Eternity* (New York, Charles Scribner's Sons, 1951).
——, *The Thin Red Line* (New York, Charles Scribner's Sons, 1962).
Kahn, Lawrence H., *Able One Four* (Denver [Colo.], Alan Swallow, 1952).
Kantor, MacKinley, *Don't Touch Me* (New York, Random House, 1951).
Kee, Robert, *A Crowd is not Company* (Garden City [N. Y.], Doubleday and Company, 1947).
Kendrick, Baynard H., *Lights Out* (New York, William Morrow and Co., 1945).
Kernan, Thomas D., *Now With the Morning Star* (New York, Charles Scribner's Sons, 1944).
Killens, John O., *And Then We Heard the Thunder* (New York, A. A. Knopf, 1962).
Klass, Joe, *Maybe I'm Dead* (New York, The Macmillan Co., 1955).
Kolb, Avery E., *Jigger Whitchet's War* (New York, Simon and Schuster, 1959).

LaFarge, Christopher, *East by Southwest* (New York, Coward-McCann, 1944).

Lakin, Richard, *The Body Fell on Berlin* (New York, G. P. Putnam's Sons, 1943).

Landon, Joseph, *Angle of Attack* (Garden City [N. Y.], Doubleday and Company, 1952).

Lay, Bierne, *Twelve O'Clock High!* (New York, Harper and Brothers, 1948).

Leonard, George, *Shoulder the Sky* (New York, McDowell, 1959).

Levin, Dan, *Mask of Glory* (New York, Whittlesay House, 1949).

Levitt, Saul, *The Sun is Silent* (New York, Harper and Brothers, 1951).

Linakis, Steven, *In the Spring the War Ended* (New York, G. P. Putnam's Sons, 1965).

Litten, Frederic N., *Rendezvous on Mindanao* (New York, Dodd, Mead & Co., 1945).

Lodwick, John, *Aegean Adventure* (New York, Dodd, Mead & Co., 1946).

——, *Running to Paradise* (New York, Dodd, Mead & Co., 1943).

Loomis, Edward, *End of a War* (New York, Ballantine Books, 1958).

Loos, Mary, *Return to the Vineyard* (Garden City [N. Y.], Doubleday, Doran & Co., 1945).

Lowry, Robert James, *Casualty* (New York, New Directions, 1946).

Lyon, Allan, *Toward an Unknown Station* (New York, The Macmillan Co., 1948).

MacCuish, David, *Do Not Go Gentle* (New York, Doubleday and Company, 1960).

Mailer, Howard, *Undertow* (Garden City [N. Y.], Doubleday, Doran & Co., 1945).

Mailer, Norman, *The Naked and the Dead* (New York, Rinehart & Co., Inc., 1948).

Mandel, George, *The War Boom* (New York, Random House, 1962).

March, Anthony, *Quit for the Next* (New York, Charles Scribner's Sons, 1945).

Marek, Stephen, *Laughter in Hell* (Caldwell [Idaho], Caxton Printers, Ltd., 1956).

Marquand, John P., *Melville Goodwin, USA* (Boston [Mass.], Little, Brown, 1951).

Marshall, Bruce, *Vespers in Vienna* (Boston, Houghton Mifflin Co., 1947).

Massian, Alexander, *Rotation* (New York, Exposition Press, Inc., 1955).

Matheson, Richard, *The Beardless Warriors* (Boston, Little, Brown, 1960).

Matthiessen, Peter, *Reditzer* (New York, The Viking Press, 1961).

McHugh, Vincent, *Edge of the World* (New York, Ballantine Books, 1950).

McLaughlin, Robert, *The Side of the Angels* (New York, A. A. Knopf, 1947).

McSwigan, Marie, *Snow Treasure* (New York, E. P. Dutton, 1942).

Mergendahl, Charles H., *Don't Wait for Spring* (Boston [Mass.], Little, Brown, 1944).

Merrick, Elliott, *Passing By* (New York, The Macmillan Co., 1947).

Merrick, Gordon, *The Strumpet Wind* (New York, William Morrow and Co., 1947).

Michener, James A., *Sayonara* (New York, Random House, 1954).
——, *Tales of the South Pacific* (New York, The Macmillan Co., 1947).
Midlam, Don S., *Flight of the "Lucky Lady"* (Portland [Ore.], Binfords & Mort, 1954).
Miller, Merle, *Island 49* (New York, Thomas Y. Crowell Co., 1945).
Moore, Brian, *The Emperor of Ice Cream* (New York, The Viking Press, 1965).
Morrill, George, *Dark Sea Running* (New York, McGraw Hill, 1959).
Moss, Sidney, *Thy Men Shall Fall* (Chicago, Ziff-Davis Publishing Co., 1948).
Mydans, Shelly S., *The Open City* (Garden City [N. Y.], Doubleday, Doran & Co., Inc., 1945).
Myrer, Anton, *The Big War* (New York, Bantam Books, 1958).
Newman, Robert H., *Far from Home* (New York, J. B. Lippincott Co., 1941).
Nicholson, Jane, *Shelter* (New York, The Viking Press, 1941).
O'Rourke, Frank, *"E" Company* (New York, Simon and Schuster, 1945).
Osler, William, *Premature Angel* (Philadelphia [Pa.], Dorrance & Co., Inc., 1954).
Palmer, Bernard A., *Dangerous Mission* (Grand Rapids [Mich.], Zendervan Publishing House, 1945).
Paul, Louis, *This is my Brother* (New York, Crown Publishers, 1943).
Pittenger, Ted, *Warrior's Return* (New York, Signet Books, 1955).
Plagemann, Bentz, *Steel Cocoon* (New York, The Viking Press, 1959).
Powell, Richard P., *The Soldier* (New York, Charles Scribner's Sons, 1960).
Prat, Rex K., *You Tell My Son* (New York, Random House, 1958).
Pratt, Theodore, *Mr. Winkle Goes to War* (New York, Duell, Sloan, & Pearce, 1943).
Prokosch, Frederic, *Age of Thunder* (New York, Harper and Brothers, 1945).
Pruett, Henry R., *Soft as Steel* (Boston [Mass.], Christopher Publishing House, 1950).
Purcell, John P., *Class Report* (New York, The Vanguard Press, 1947).
Redding, John M., and Thor Smith, *Wake of Glory* (New York, Bobbs-Merrill, 1945).
Reed, Kit, *At War as Children* (New York, Farrar, Straus, 1964).
Reynolds, Quentin J., *Known But to God* (New York, Day, 1960).
——, *The Man who Wouldn't Talk* (New York, Random House, 1953).
Ritchie, Lewis, *Action Stations* (Boston [Mass.], Little, Brown, 1941).
Roberts, Cecil, *The Labyrinth* (Garden City [N. Y.], Doubleday, Doran and Co., Inc., 1944).
Robinson, Wayne, *Barbara* (New York, Doubleday and Company, 1961).
Rochard, Henri, *I Was a Male War Bride* (Califon [N. J.], Montgrove Press, 1955).
Ross, James E., *The Dead Are Mine* (New York, McKay, 1963).
Rubenstein, S. Leonard, *The Battle Done* (New York, William Morrow and Co., Inc., 1954).

176 BIBLIOGRAPHY

St. John, Robert, *It's Always Tomorrow* (Garden City [N. Y.], Doubleday, Doran and Co., Inc., 1944).

Scannell, Francis P., *In Line of Duty* (New York, Harper and Brothers, 1946).

Scott, John F., *The Earth Is Laughing* (New York, Exposition Press Inc., 1956).

Sedgwick, Alexander C., *Tell Sparta* (Boston [Mass.], Houghton Mifflin Co., 1945).

Shaw, Irwin, *The Young Lions* (New York, Random House, 1948).

Sheldon, Walt, *Troubling of a Star* (New York, J. B. Lippincott Co., 1953).

Sire, Glen, *The Deathmakers* (New York, Simon and Schuster, 1960).

Skidmore, Hobert D., *Valley of the Sky* (Boston [Mass.], Houghton Mifflin Co., 1944).

Slote, A., *Strangers and Comrades* (New York, Simon and Schuster, 1964).

Smith, William C., *Last of the Conquerors* (New York, Farrar, Straus & Cudahy, 1948).

Spaulding, Charles F., and Otis Carney, *Love at First Flight* (Boston [Mass.], Houghton Mifflin Co., 1943).

Stern, Richard G., *In Any Case* (New York, McGraw Hill, 1962).

Stewart, Catherine P., *So Thick the Fog* (New York, Charles Scribner's Sons, 1944).

Stiles, Bert, *Serenade to the Big Bird* (New York, W. W. Norton & Co., Inc., 1952).

Strachey, John, *The Frontiers* (New York, Random House, 1952).

Syers, William E., *The Seven: Navy Subchaser* (New York, Duell, Sloan, 1960).

Sykes, Gerald, *Nice American* (New York, Farrar, Straus & Cudahy, 1951).

Szymczak, Chester A., *When Time Stood Still* (Philadelphia [Pa.], Dorrance & Co., Inc., 1956).

Taylor, Jim, *Bring Your Own Thirst* (Philadelphia [Pa.], Dorrance & Co., Inc., 1953).

Taylor, Ward, *Roll Back the Sky* (New York, Henry Holt and Co., 1956).

Tedford, Paul, *No More Mud* (Philadelphia [Pa.], Dorrance & Co., Inc., 1952).

Teilhet, Hildegarde, *The Double Agent* (Garden City [N. Y.], Doubleday, Doran & Co., Inc., 1945).

Thacher, Russell, *The Captain* (New York, The Macmillan Co., 1951).

——, *Break in the Clouds* (New York, J. B. Lippincott Co., 1957).

Towner, Wesley, *The Liberators* (New York, A. A. Wyn, 1946).

Tralins, S. Robert, *Corporal Glory* (New York, Exposition Press, Inc., 1953).

Tregaskis, Richard, *Stronger than Fear* (New York, Random House, 1945).

Uris, Leon M., *The Angry Hills* (New York, Random House, 1955).

——, *Battlecry* (New York, G. P. Putnam's Sons, 1953).

Van Loon, Hendrik W., *Invasion* (New York, Harcourt, Brace and Co., 1940).

Van Praag, Van, *Day Without End* (New York, W. Sloane Associates, 1949).

Vidal, Gore, *Williwaw* (New York, E. P. Dutton, 1946).
Viertel, Peter, *Line of Departure* (New York, Harcourt, Brace and Co., 1947).
Wadelton, T. D., *Silver Buckles on His Knee* (New York, Coward McCann, 1945).
Wakeman, Frederic, *Shore Leave* (New York, Signet Books, 1948).
Wallenstein, Marcel H., *Red Canvas* (New York, Creative Age Press, Inc., 1946).
Waller, Leslie, *Show Me the Way* (New York, The Viking Press, 1947).
——, *Three-Day Pass* (New York, The Viking Press, 1945).
Webber, Gordon, *The Far Shore* (Boston [Mass.], Little, Brown, 1954).
Weller, George A., *The Crack in the Column* (New York, Random House, 1949).
Wernick, Robert, *The Freebooters* (New York, Charles Scribner's Sons, 1949).
Westheimer, David, *Von Ryan's Express* (New York, Doubleday and Company, 1963).
Wheatley, Dennis, *Faked Passports* (New York, The Macmillan Co., 1943).
——, *V for Vengeance* (New York, The Macmillan Co., 1942).
White, Marion, *If We Should Fail* (New York, M. S. Mill Co., Inc., 1942).
White, Theodore H., *The Mountain Road* (New York, William Sloane Associates, 1958).
Willets, Ann, *Sting of Glory* (New York, Random House, 1954).
Williams, Wirt, *The Enemy* (Boston [Mass.], Houghton Mifflin Co., 1951).
Williamson, Scott G., *A Convoy Through the Dream* (New York, The Macmillan Co., 1948).
Wilson, Sloan, *Voyage to Somewhere* (New York, A. A. Wyn, 1946).
Wolfert, Ira, *An Act of Love* (New York, Simon and Schuster, 1948).
Woods, William H., *The Edge of Darkness* (New York, J. B. Lippincott Co., 1942).
——, *The Street of Seven Monks* (Boston, Little, Brown, 1948).
Wouk, Herman, *The Caine Mutiny* (Garden City [N. Y.], Doubleday and Company, 1951).

AUTHOR-TITLE INDEX